MASTER THE™ DSST®

Money and Banking Exam

About Peterson's®

Peterson's has been your trusted educational publisher for over 50 years. It's a milestone we're quite proud of, as we continue to offer the most accurate, dependable, high-quality educational content in the field, providing you with everything you need to succeed. No matter where you are on your academic or professional path, you can rely on Peterson's for its books, online information, expert test-prep tools, the most up-to-date education exploration data, and the highest quality career success resources—everything you need to achieve your education goals. For our complete line of products, visit **www.petersons.com.**

For more information, contact Peterson's, 4380 S. Syracuse St., Suite 200, Denver, CO 80237; 800-338-3282 Ext. 54229; or visit us online at **www.petersons.com.**

ISBN: 978-0-7689-4464-8

Printed in the United States of America

10 9 8 7 6 5 4 3 2 1   22 21 20

Contents

Before You Begin

HOW THIS BOOK IS ORGANIZED

Peterson's *Master the*™ *DSST® Money and Banking Exam* provides a diagnostic test, subject-matter review, and a post-test.

- **Diagnostic Test**—Twenty multiple-choice questions, followed by an answer key with detailed answer explanations
- **Assessment Grid**—A chart designed to help you identify areas that you need to focus on based on your test results
- **Subject-Matter Review**—General overview of the exam subject, followed by a review of the relevant topics and terminology covered on the exam
- **Post-test**—Sixty multiple-choice questions, followed by an answer key and detailed answer explanations

The purpose of the diagnostic test is to help you figure out what you know—or don't know. The twenty multiple-choice questions are similar to the ones found on the DSST exam, and they should provide you with a good idea of what to expect. Once you take the diagnostic test, check your answers to see how you did. Included with each correct answer is a brief explanation regarding why a specific answer is correct, and in many cases, why other options are incorrect. Use the assessment grid to identify the questions you miss so that you can spend more time reviewing that information later. As with any exam, knowing your weak spots greatly improves your chances of success.

Following the diagnostic test is a subject-matter review. The review summarizes the various topics covered on the DSST exam. Key terms are defined; important concepts are explained; and when appropriate, examples are provided. As you read the review, some of the information may seem familiar while other information may seem foreign. Again, take note of the unfamiliar because that will most likely cause you problems on the actual exam.

After studying the subject-matter review, you should be ready for the post-test. The post-test contains sixty multiple-choice items, and it will serve as a dry run for the real DSST exam. There are complete answer explanations at the end of the test.

OTHER DSST® PRODUCTS BY PETERSON'S

Books, flashcards, practice tests, and videos available online at **www.petersons.com/testprep/dsst**

- A History of the Vietnam War
- Art of the Western World
- Astronomy
- Business Mathematics
- Business Ethics and Society
- Civil War and Reconstruction
- Computing and Information Technology
- Criminal Justice
- Environmental Science
- Ethics in America
- Ethics in Technology
- Foundations of Education
- Fundamentals of College Algebra
- Fundamentals of Counseling
- Fundamentals of Cybersecurity
- General Anthropology
- Health and Human Development
- History of the Soviet Union
- Human Resource Management
- Introduction to Business
- Introduction to Geography
- Introduction to Geology
- Introduction to Law Enforcement
- Introduction to World Religions
- Lifespan Developmental Psychology
- Math for Liberal Arts
- Management Information Systems
- Money and Banking
- Organizational Behavior
- Personal Finance
- Principles of Advanced English Composition
- Principles of Finance
- Principles of Public Speaking
- Principles of Statistics
- Principles of Supervision
- Substance Abuse
- Technical Writing

Like what you see? Get unlimited access to Peterson's full catalog of DSST practice tests, instructional videos, flashcards, and more for **75% off the first month!** Go to **www.petersons.com/testprep/dsst** and use coupon code **DSST2020** at checkout. Offer expires July 1, 2021.

Chapter 1

All About the DSST® Exam

WHAT IS THE DSST®?

Previously known as the DANTES Subject Standardized Tests, the DSST program provides the opportunity for individuals to earn college credit for what they have learned outside of the traditional classroom. Accepted or administered at more than 1,900 colleges and universities nationwide and approved by the American Council on Education (ACE), the DSST program enables individuals to use the knowledge they have acquired outside the classroom to accomplish their educational and professional goals.

WHY TAKE A DSST® EXAM?

DSST exams offer a way for you to save both time and money in your quest for a college education. Why enroll in a college course in a subject you already understand? For more than 30 years, the DSST program has offered the perfect solution for individuals who are knowledgeable in a specific subject and want to save both time and money. A passing score on a DSST exam provides physical evidence to universities of proficiency in a specific subject. More than 1,900 accredited and respected colleges and universities across the nation award undergraduate credit for passing scores on DSST exams. With the DSST program, individuals can shave months off the time it takes to earn a degree.

The DSST program offers numerous advantages for individuals in all stages of their educational development:

- Adult learners
- College students
- Military personnel

Adult learners desiring college degrees face unique circumstances— demanding work schedules, family responsibilities, and tight budgets. Yet

1

adult learners also have years of valuable work experience that can frequently be applied toward a degree through the DSST program. For example, adult learners with on-the-job experience in business and management might be able to skip the Business 101 courses if they earn passing marks on DSST exams such as Introduction to Business and Principles of Supervision.

Adult learners can put their prior learning into action and move forward with more advanced course work. Adults who have never enrolled in a college course may feel a little uncertain about their abilities. If this describes your situation, then sign up for a DSST exam and see how you do. A passing score may be the boost you need to realize your dream of earning a degree. With family and work commitments, adult learners often feel they lack the time to attend college. The DSST program provides adult learners with the unique opportunity to work toward college degrees without the time constraints of semester-long course work. DSST exams take two hours or less to complete. In one weekend, you could earn credit for multiple college courses.

The DSST exams also benefit students who are already enrolled in a college or university. With college tuition costs on the rise, most students face financial challenges. The fee for each DSST exam starts at $85 (plus administration fees charged by some testing facilities)—significantly less than the $750 average cost of a 3-hour college class. Maximize tuition assistance by taking DSST exams for introductory or mandatory course work. Once you earn a passing score on a DSST exam, you are free to move on to higher-level course work in that subject matter, take desired electives, or focus on courses in a chosen major.

Not only do college students and adult learners profit from DSST exams, but military personnel reap the benefits as well. If you are a member of the armed services at home or abroad, you can initiate your post-military career by taking DSST exams in areas with which you have experience. Military personnel can gain credit anywhere in the world, thanks to the fact that almost all of the tests are available through the internet at designated testing locations. DSST testing facilities are located at over 500 military installations, so service members on active duty can get a jump-start on a post-military career with the DSST program. As an additional incentive, DANTES (Defense Activity for Non-Traditional Education Support) provides funding for DSST test fees for eligible members of the military.

Over 30 subject-matter tests are available in the fields of Business, Humanities, Math, Physical Science, Social Sciences, and Technology.

Available DSST® Exams

Business	Social Sciences
Business Ethics and Society	A History of the Vietnam War
Business Mathematics	Art of the Western World
Computing and Information Technology	Criminal Justice
Human Resource Management	Foundations of Education
Introduction to Business	Fundamentals of Counseling
Management Information Systems	General Anthropology
Money and Banking	History of the Soviet Union
Organizational Behavior	Introduction to Geography
Personal Finance	Introduction to Law Enforcement
Principles of Finance	Lifespan Developmental Psychology
Principles of Supervision	Substance Abuse
	The Civil War and Reconstruction

Humanities	Physical Science
Ethics in America	Astronomy
Introduction to World Religions	Environmental Science
Principles of Advanced English Composition	Health and Human Development
Principles of Public Speaking	Introduction to Geology

Math	Technology
Fundamentals of College Algebra	Ethics in Technology
Math for Liberal Arts	Fundamentals of Cybersecurity
Principles of Statistics	Technical Writing

As you can see from the table, the DSST program covers a wide variety of subjects. However, it is important to ask two questions before registering for a DSST exam.

1. Which universities or colleges award credit for passing DSST exams?
2. Which DSST exams are the most relevant to my desired degree and my experience?

Knowing which universities offer DSST credit is important. In all likelihood, a college in your area awards credit for DSST exams, but find out before taking an exam by contacting the university directly. Then review the list of DSST exams to determine which ones are most relevant to the degree you are seeking and to your base of knowledge. Schedule an appointment with your college adviser to determine which exams best fit your degree program and which college courses the DSST exams can replace. Advisers should also be able to tell you the minimum score required on the DSST exam to receive university credit.

DSST® TEST CENTERS

You can find DSST testing locations in community colleges and universities across the country. Check the DSST website (**www.getcollegecredit. com**) for a location near you or contact your local college or university to find out if the school administers DSST exams. Keep in mind that some universities and colleges administer DSST exams only to enrolled students. DSST testing is available to men and women in the armed services at more than 500 military installations around the world.

HOW TO REGISTER FOR A DSST® EXAM

Once you have located a nearby DSST testing facility, you need to contact the testing center to find out the exam administration schedule. Many centers are set up to administer tests via the internet, while others use printed materials. Almost all DSST exams are available as online tests, but the method used depends on the testing center. The cost for each DSST exam starts at $85, and many testing locations charge a fee to cover their costs for administering the tests. Credit cards are the only accepted payment method for taking online DSST exams. Credit card, certified check, and money order are acceptable payment methods for paper-and-pencil tests.

Test takers are allotted two score reports—one mailed to them and another mailed to a designated college or university, if requested. Online tests generate unofficial scores at the end of the test session, while individuals taking paper tests must wait four to six weeks for score reports.

PREPARING FOR A DSST® EXAM

Even though you are knowledgeable in a certain subject matter, you should still prepare for the test to ensure you achieve the highest score possible. The first step in studying for a DSST exam is to find out what will be on the specific test you have chosen. Information regarding test content is located on the DSST fact sheets, which can be downloaded at no cost from **www.getcollegecredit.com**. Each fact sheet outlines the topics covered on a subject-matter test, as well as the approximate percentage assigned to each topic. For example, questions on the Money and Banking exam are distributed in the following way: the Roles and Kinds of Money-5%, Commercial Banks and Other Financial Intermediaries-25%, Money and Macroeconomic Activity-19%, Central Banking and the Federal Reserve System-18%, Monetary Policy in the United States-20%, and the International Monetary System-10%.

In addition to the breakdown of topics on a DSST exam, the fact sheet also lists recommended reference materials. If you do not own the recommended books, then check college bookstores. Avoid paying high prices for new textbooks by looking online for used textbooks. Don't panic if you are unable to locate a specific textbook listed on the fact sheet; the textbooks are merely recommendations. Instead, search for comparable books used in university courses on the specific subject. Current editions are ideal, and it is a good idea to use at least two references when studying for a DSST exam. Of course, the subject matter provided in this book will be a sufficient review for most test takers. However, if you need additional information, then it is a good idea to have some of the reference materials at your disposal when preparing for a DSST exam.

Fact sheets include other useful information in addition to a list of reference materials and topics. Each fact sheet includes subject-specific sample questions like those you will encounter on the DSST exam. The sample questions provide an idea of the types of questions you can expect on the exam. Test questions are multiple-choice with one correct answer and three incorrect choices.

The fact sheet also includes information about the number of credit hours ACE has recommended be awarded by colleges for a passing DSST exam score. However, you should keep in mind that not all universities and colleges adhere to the ACE recommendation for DSST credit hours. Some institutions require DSST exam scores higher than the minimum score recommended by ACE. Once you have acquired appropriate reference materials and you have the outline provided on the fact sheet, you are ready to start studying, which is where this book can help.

TEST DAY

After reviewing the material and taking practice tests, you are finally ready to take your DSST exam. Follow these tips for a successful test day experience.

1. **Arrive on time.** Not only is it courteous to arrive on time to the DSST testing facility, but it also allows plenty of time for you to take care of check-in procedures and settle into your surroundings.

2. **Bring identification.** DSST test facilities require that candidates bring a valid government-issued identification card with a current photo and signature. Acceptable forms of identification include a current driver's license, passport, military identification card, or state-issued identification card. Individuals who fail to bring proper identification to the DSST testing facility will not be allowed to take an exam.

3. **Bring the right supplies.** If your exam requires the use of a calculator, you may bring a calculator that meets the specifications. For paper-based exams, you may also bring No. 2 pencils with an eraser and black ballpoint pens. Regardless of the exam methodology, you are NOT allowed to bring reference or study materials, scratch paper, or electronics such as cell phones, personal handheld devices, cameras, alarm wrist watches, or tape recorders to the testing center.

4. **Take the test.** During the exam, take the time to read each question-and-answer option carefully. Eliminate the choices you know are incorrect to narrow the number of potential answers. If a question completely stumps you, take an educated guess and move on—remember that DSSTs are timed; you will have 2 hours to take the exam.

With the proper preparation, DSST exams will save you both time and money. So join the thousands of people who have already reaped the benefits of DSST exams and move closer than ever to your college degree.

MONEY AND BANKING EXAM FACTS

The DSST® Money and Banking exam consists of 100 multiple-choice questions that cover material commonly found in a college-level money and banking course, including the role of money, types of money, commercial banks, the Federal Reserve System, macroeconomics, US monetary policy, and the international monetary system.

Area or Course Equivalent: Money and Banking
Level: Lower-level baccalaureate
Amount of Credit: 3 Semester Hours
Minimum Score: 400
Source: www.getcollegecredit.com/wp-content/assets/factsheets/MoneyAndBanking.pdf

I. **The Roles and Kinds of Money – 5%**

a. Alternative definitions of money

b. Money and other assets

II. Commercial Banks and Other Financial Intermediaries – 28%

    a. Regulation of the banking industry

    b. Structure of the banking industry

    c. Operation and management of financial markets and intermediaries

    d. Deposit insurance

III. Money and Macroeconomic Activity – 19%

    a. Basic classical and Keynesian economics

    b. Monetarism and rational expectations

    c. Money and inflation

IV. Central Banking and the Federal Reserve System – 18%

    a. Historical and philosophical framework

    b. Structure and organization

    c. Current monetary management

V. Monetary Policy in the United States – 20%

    a. Policy effectiveness

    b. Conducting monetary policy

    c. Interest rates and the impact on money supply

    d. Monetary vs. fiscal policy

    e. The financial crisis of 2008/2009

VI. The International Monetary System – 10%

    a. International banking

    b. International monetary institutions and debt crisis

    c. International payments and exchange rates

    d. Monetary policy in conjunction with exchange rate

Chapter 2

Money and Banking Diagnostic Test

DIAGNOSTIC TEST ANSWER SHEET

1. Ⓐ Ⓑ Ⓒ Ⓓ
2. Ⓐ Ⓑ Ⓒ Ⓓ
3. Ⓐ Ⓑ Ⓒ Ⓓ
4. Ⓐ Ⓑ Ⓒ Ⓓ
5. Ⓐ Ⓑ Ⓒ Ⓓ
6. Ⓐ Ⓑ Ⓒ Ⓓ
7. Ⓐ Ⓑ Ⓒ Ⓓ
8. Ⓐ Ⓑ Ⓒ Ⓓ

9. Ⓐ Ⓑ Ⓒ Ⓓ
10. Ⓐ Ⓑ Ⓒ Ⓓ
11. Ⓐ Ⓑ Ⓒ Ⓓ
12. Ⓐ Ⓑ Ⓒ Ⓓ
13. Ⓐ Ⓑ Ⓒ Ⓓ
14. Ⓐ Ⓑ Ⓒ Ⓓ
15. Ⓐ Ⓑ Ⓒ Ⓓ
16. Ⓐ Ⓑ Ⓒ Ⓓ

17. Ⓐ Ⓑ Ⓒ Ⓓ
18. Ⓐ Ⓑ Ⓒ Ⓓ
19. Ⓐ Ⓑ Ⓒ Ⓓ
20. Ⓐ Ⓑ Ⓒ Ⓓ

MONEY AND BANKING DIAGNOSTIC TEST

24 minutes—20 questions

Directions: Carefully read each of the following 20 questions. Choose the best answer to each question and fill in the corresponding circle on the answer sheet. The Answer Key and Explanations can be found following this Diagnostic Test.

---

1. *Fiat money* is the term used for a means of payment that

    A. can be converted into gold at any time.
    B. is widely accepted because it's made of precious metals like silver or gold.
    C. cannot be accepted as repayment of a debt.
    D. is not backed by any commodity.

2. Up until 1994, nationwide branch banking was prohibited by

    A. Regulation Q and the Glass-Steagall Act.
    B. the McFadden Act.
    C. the Depository Institutions Deregulation and Monetary Control Act.
    D. the Riegle-Neal Interstate Banking Act.

3. When an American money market mutual fund purchases US Treasury notes from an American bank, the transaction is

    A. not counted in the Gross Domestic Product for the current period.
    B. counted in the Gross Domestic Product in the financial account.
    C. counted in the Gross Domestic Product under Gross Private Investment.
    D. counted in the Balance of Payment in the financial account.

4. The Federal Reserve Bank was created primarily to

    A. maintain the stability of the financial system by providing liquidity and acting as lender of last resort to member banks.
    B. maintain the stability of the banking sector by providing insurance to depositors' accounts.
    C. prevent any form of discrimination toward women and minorities in all aspects of credit transactions.
    D. enforce macro-prudential regulation that would help contain systemic risk.

5. A financial intermediary has a liquidity problem when

A. its liabilities exceed the bank's assets.
B. its asset portfolio is predominantly composed of Treasury securities that the intermediary can easily sell to other financial institutions.
C. it has cash assets in excess of its required reserves.
D. its current obligations exceed the institution's current liquid resources.

6. Central banks do not have complete control over the money supply because

A. they do not fully control the money multiplier.
B. they do not have the legal authority to set reserve requirements.
C. they prefer controlling the monetary base.
D. the policy interest rate does not influence the money supply.

7. A downside of having the FDIC insure deposit accounts up to $250,000 is the

A. increase in financial contagion.
B. increase in banks' holdings of excess reserves.
C. decrease in market discipline.
D. decrease in bank failures.

8. One difference between classical economists and Keynesian economists is that Keynesian economists believe that

A. prices are flexible and absorb all shocks in demand and supply.
B. higher investment spending can raise the level of output.
C. the economy is always at full employment and any worker out of job is voluntarily unemployed.
D. lower interest rates and a higher money supply tend to reduce the price level.

9. Unlike an expansionary fiscal policy, an expansionary monetary policy lowers

A. total spending.
B. taxes.
C. interest rates.
D. government purchases.

10. According to the quantity theory of money, a continual increase of the money supply leads to inflation because

   A. real GDP is below potential output.
   B. interest rates are sticky.
   C. the foreign exchange rate is overvalued.
   D. the velocity of money is constant.

11. Each year, the Federal Open Market Committee (FOMC) has eight regular meetings. Which of the following is decided at the regular meetings of the FOMC?

   A. The reserve requirement imposed on member banks
   B. The target level of the Federal Funds Rate
   C. The discount rate charged in each of the twelve Reserve districts
   D. The target level of the monetary aggregate M2

12. Monetarists believe that firms, workers, and investors have rational expectations and that

   A. the price level they expect is not sensitive to the money supply.
   B. they suffer from monetary illusion.
   C. monetizing the public deficits would lower inflation.
   D. only monetary policy can contain inflation.

13. An advantage of requiring borrowers to post collateral when they apply for a loan is that it

   A. helps bank reach a wider public and better meet the Equal Credit Opportunity Act requirements.
   B. increases borrowers' incentive to apply for loans.
   C. lowers borrowers' incentive to take up excessive risk.
   D. attracts borrowers with a poorer credit history who are willing to pay higher interest rates.

14. The different channels through which monetary policy influences economic activity are called the

   A. transmission mechanism.
   B. equation of exchange.
   C. automatic stabilizers.
   D. monetary lags.

15. A distinctive feature of the banking sector of the United States is the

    A. even geographical distribution of commercial banks and Savings and Loans Associations.

    B. prevalence among depository institutions of member owned credit unions.

    C. existence of a limited number of very large bank holdings among thousands of relatively small commercial banks.

    D. highly restricted range of bank activities allowed to Savings and Loans Associations.

16. Which of the following is a function of the International Monetary Fund (IMF)?

    A. Promoting international cooperation among monetary authorities and financial supervisory officials

    B. Providing development loans so as to end extreme poverty

    C. Promoting smooth and free international trade flows

    D. Providing loans to countries with balance of payment difficulties or facing debt crises

17. When the Federal Reserve lowers the federal funds rate, banks

    A. would rather borrow from the Federal Reserve at the discount rate than from each other at the lower federal funds rate.

    B. can borrow reserves more cheaply than before and are more likely to extend new loans so that the money supply increases.

    C. find it harder to meet reserve requirements and increase their holdings of excess reserves.

    D. become aware of the new policy only if it is clearly announced at the end of the FOMC meeting.

18. A Certificate of Deposit differs from a Money Market Deposit Account in that a

    A. money market deposit account is not FDIC insured.

    B. certificate of deposit will give you access to your funds at a specified time in the future.

    C. certificate of deposit does not pay interest.

    D. money market deposit account is a bank liability, while a CD is a bank asset.

19. Which of the following statements best characterizes the Federal Reserve's response to the financial crisis of 2008/2009?

A. Concerned that injecting liquidity in the largest banks could worsen existing problems of moral hazard, the Federal Reserve took a hands-off approach and allowed these institutions to fail.

B. According to the principle that acute crises can have a cleansing effect on financial markets, the Federal Reserve allowed larger commercial banks to fail; however, to contain systemic risk, it supported smaller banks.

C. The Federal Reserve lowered the federal funds rate down to the zero lower bound and found itself with no other tools it could use to inject liquidity in the banking sector and in money markets.

D. The Federal Reserve lowered the federal funds rate and used unconventional monetary tools like large purchases of Mortgage Back Securities from Government Sponsored Entities to stimulate the housing market.

20. After President Kennedy created the United States Agency for International Development (USAID), US foreign aid to other countries sharply increased,

A. raising debits in the US current account of the Balance of Payment.

B. raising credits in the US current account of the Balance of Payment.

C. raising debits in the US financial account of the Balance of Payment.

D. raising credits in the US financial account of the Balance of Payment.

ANSWER KEY AND EXPLANATIONS

1. D	5. D	9. C	13. C	17. B
2. B	6. A	10. D	14. A	18. B
3. A	7. C	11. B	15. C	19. D
4. A	8. B	12. D	16. D	20. A

1. **The correct answer is D.** Unlike commodity money, fiat money is not backed by anything. Fiat money has value because people trust that it will be widely accepted as a means of payment now and in the future. Choice A is incorrect because money that can be converted into gold is called commodity-backed money. Choice B is incorrect because money made of precious metal is called commodity money. Choice C is incorrect because fiat money is currency that the government has declared legal tender.

2. **The correct answer is B.** The McFadden Act of 1927 required national banks to open branches only according to the laws of the state where they were located, effectively prohibiting national branching. Regulation Q (choice A) imposed limits on interest paid on various deposits, and prohibited paying interest on demand deposits. The DIDMCA (choice C) did not prohibit nationwide branching, but, among other things, lifted restrictions on interest paid on deposits. The Riegle-Neal Interstate Banking Act (choice D) removed the restrictions on nationwide branching.

3. **The correct answer is A.** Gross Domestic Product only counts transactions of final goods and services. Choice B is incorrect because the financial account is not a component of Gross Domestic Product. Choice C is incorrect because purchases of US Treasury notes are a form of financial investment, not of Gross Private Investment. Choice D is incorrect because the purchase is a domestic transaction.

4. **The correct answer is A.** The Federal Reserve System was created to provide elastic liquidity to the banking sector and act as a lender of last resort to member banks so as to maintain financial stability. Choice B is incorrect because bank deposits are insured by the FDIC and other agencies, not by the Federal Reserve Bank. Choice C is incorrect because discrimination in lending was outlawed by the Equal Credit Opportunity Act in 1974. Choice D is incorrect because the Federal Reserve Bank started enforcing macro-prudential regulation in response to the financial crises of 2008.

5. **The correct answer is D.** A financial intermediary has a liquidity problem if it does not hold enough liquid resources like cash or Treasury securities to meet its current obligation, which can include short-term debt or depositors' withdrawals. Choice A is incorrect because when a financial intermediary's liabilities exceed its assets the intermediary is insolvent. Choice B is incorrect because assets that can be easily sold are very liquid. Choice C is incorrect because not all financial intermediaries are subject to reserve requirements.

6. **The correct answer is A.** Money supply is sensitive to changes in the monetary base and the money multiplier and central banks do not fully control the money multiplier. Choice B is incorrect because central banks set reserve requirements. Choice C is incorrect because central banks want to influence money supply while the monetary base is an intermediate target. Choice D is incorrect because the money supply is sensitive to the policy interest rate.

7. **The correct answer is C.** Deposit insurance reduces depositors' incentive to monitor the sound management of their banks, reducing market discipline. Choice A is incorrect because deposit insurance prevents financial contagion. Choice B is incorrect because deposit insurance reduces the chances of a bank run and banks' incentive to hold excess reserves. Choice D is incorrect because a decrease in bank failures is an upside of deposit insurance.

8. **The correct answer is B.** Keynesian economists believe that prices are sticky and output follows total spending so that higher investment spending can raise output. Choice A is incorrect because it's classical economists who believe that prices are flexible. Choice C is incorrect because Keynesian economists believe that when total spending drops because of sticky prices and wages many workers become involuntarily unemployed. Choice D is incorrect because both theories support that a higher money supply increases the price level.

9. **The correct answer is C.** An expansionary monetary policy lowers interest rates to stimulate investment and consumption while an expansionary fiscal policy increases the public deficit leading to higher interest rates. Choice A is incorrect because an expansionary monetary policy aims at increasing total spending. Choice B is incorrect because taxes are a tool of fiscal policy. Choice D is incorrect because government purchases are a tool of fiscal policy.

10. **The correct answer is D.** The quantity theory of money states that money and prices are linked by the equation of exchange $P \times Y = M \times V$ and assumes that V and Y are constant so that changes in the money supply lead to equal changes in the price level. Choice A is incorrect because the quantity theory of money assumes that the economy is always at full employment. Choice B is incorrect because the quantity theory of money is silent on interest rates. Choice C is incorrect because the quantity theory of money does not take into account the foreign exchange market.

11. **The correct answer is B.** At its regular meetings, the FOMC discusses the current economic outlook and decides the target level of the Federal Funds Rate. Choice A is incorrect because reserve requirements are decided by the Board of Governors. Choice C is incorrect because the discount rates charged by the Reserve banks are decided by the individual banks under the control of the Board of Governors. Choice D is incorrect because the US monetary policy uses the Federal Funds Rate as its policy target, not the monetary aggregate M2.

12. **The correct answer is D.** Monetarists believe that, because market participants have rational expectations, fiscal policy is ineffective in controlling inflation, which is a monetary phenomenon. Choice A is incorrect because according to the rational expectation hypothesis the money supply influences the price level people expect. Choice B is incorrect because when people have rational expectations, they do not suffer from monetary illusion. Choice C is incorrect because monetarists believe that printing money to pay for the public deficit increases inflation.

13. **The correct answer is C.** With collateralized loans, in the case of default, the borrower loses the collateral, leading the borrower to be more cautious when choosing how to use the funds. Choice A is incorrect because many families and small businesses do not have assets they can post as collateral, and collateral requirements reduce a bank's reach. Choice B is incorrect because posting collateral lowers a borrower's incentive to apply for a loan. Choice D is incorrect because borrowers with a poorer credit history are less likely to own assets they can post as collateral.

14. **The correct answer is A.** The transmission mechanism describes the ways in which monetary policy influences total spending and the level of economic activity. The equation of exchange (choice B) illustrates only the relationship between the money supply and the price level. Automatic stabilizers (choice C) are tools of fiscal policy. Monetary lags (choice D) describe different reasons why it takes about two years for monetary policy to influence the economy.

15. **The correct answer is C.** In the United States, most commercial banks are rather small and the 84 largest bank holdings hold more than 70 percent of all deposits. Choice A is incorrect because the geographical distribution of commercial banks is not geographically even. Choice B is incorrect because most depository institutions are commercial banks. Choice D is incorrect because, thanks to recent regulatory changes, Savings and Loans Associations can perform most of the same activities as commercial banks.

16. **The correct answer is D.** The IMF was founded to help countries with balance of payment difficulties under the Bretton Woods regime of fixed exchange rates. More recently, it acts as a lender of last resort for countries with external debt crises. Promoting international cooperation among monetary authorities and financial supervisory officials (choice A) is the key function of the Bank of International Settlements (BIS). Providing development loans to end extreme poverty (choice B) is a key function of the World Bank. Promoting smooth and free trade flows (choice C) is the key function of the World Trade Organization (WTO).

17. **The correct answer is B.** Banks extend loans when they have a cheap source of funding. A lower federal funds rate lowers banks' cost of money. Choice A is incorrect if the federal funds rate is lower than the discount rate banks would borrow in the federal funds market instead of borrowing from the Fed. Choice C is incorrect because if banks can borrow from each other more cheaply than before, they find it easier, not harder, to meet reserve requirements. Choice D is incorrect because the federal funds rate is the interest rate that banks charge each other on overnight loans of federal funds so they are directly aware of changes in the rate.

18. **The correct answer is B.** Certificates of deposit are one type of time deposits, deposits that give you access to your funds only at a specified time in the future. Choice A is incorrect because money market deposit accounts are FDIC insured up to $250,000 per account. Choice C is incorrect because certificates of deposit pay a fixed prespecified interest. Choice D is incorrect because both money market deposit accounts and certificate of deposits are types of deposits and are a bank's liabilities.

19. The correct answer is D. After lowering the federal funds rate to its zero lower bound, the Fed introduced new liquidity provisions and started large purchases of mortgage back securities and long-term Treasury securities; these are unconventional tools of monetary policy. Choice A is incorrect because the Federal Reserve did not take a hands-off approach. Choice B is incorrect because during the financial crises more than 400 banks failed, most of them smaller banks. Choice C is incorrect because the Federal Reserve used several unconventional tools to inject liquidity in the banking sector and in specific segments of the US financial markets.

20. The correct answer is A. In the Balance of Payment, foreign aid is tallied as a debit in the current account. Choice B is incorrect because in the Balance of Payment, foreign aid is tallied as a debit, not a credit. Choice C is incorrect because in the Balance of Payment, foreign aid is tallied in the current account, not the financial account. Choice D is incorrect because in the Balance of Payment, foreign aid is tallied as a debit, not a credit.

DIAGNOSTIC TEST ASSESSMENT GRID

Now that you've completed the diagnostic test and read through the answer explanations, you can use your results to target your studying. Find the question numbers from the diagnostic test that you answered incorrectly and highlight or circle them below. Then focus extra attention on the sections dealing with those topics.

Money and Banking		
Content Area	**Topic**	**Question #**
The Roles and Kinds of Money	• Alternative definitions of money • Money and other assets	1
Commercial Banks and Other Financial Intermediaries	• Regulation of the banking industry • Structure of the banking industry • Operation and management of financial markets and intermediaries • Deposit insurance	2, 5, 7, 13, 15, 18
Money and Macroeconomic Activity	• Basic classical and Keynesian economics • Monetarism and rational expectations • Money and inflation	3, 8, 10, 12
Central Banking and the Federal Reserve System	• Historical and philosophical framework • Structure and organization • Current monetary management	4, 6, 11
Monetary Policy in the United States	• Policy effectiveness • Conducting monetary policy • Interest rates and the impact on money supply • Monetary vs. fiscal policy • The financial crisis of 2008/2009	9, 14, 17, 19
The International Monetary System	• International banking • International monetary institutions and debt crisis • International payments and exchange rates • Monetary policy in conjunction with exchange rate	16, 20

Chapter 3

Money and Banking Subject Review

THE ROLES AND KINDS OF MONEY

Alternative Definitions of Money

Let's start by defining the concept of money. Money is an **asset**—a durable item with value that is widely accepted as means of payment.

Only some valuables or assets can be used as money. Assets that can be used as money are:

- **Durable:** They last over time.
- **Acceptable:** People do not find them repulsive or inconvenient to carry.
- **Divisible:** They can be divided into smaller units
- **Fungible:** Each unit is similar to every other unit so that they can be easily interchanged.

The Four Key Roles of Money

Economists find that money has four key roles:

1. *Means of payment:* Money makes it easier for buyers and sellers to come together and trade. Without money, people would have to barter, that is exchange one good for another. However, bartering requires a double coincidence of wants: If Joe wants to trade his Netflix subscription for a DSST study guide, he has to meet someone willing to trade a DSST study guide for a Netflix subscription. Because money is widely accepted as a means of payment, when Joe wants to trade money for a DSST study guide, he can easily find a bookstore willing to trade a DSST study guide for money.
2. *Store of value:* An important feature of money is that people can save it for future purchases. If snowballs were used as money, our wages would melt before we could spend them.

3. *Standard of deferred payment:* Money is the unit we use to agree on the future repayment of a debt. In the United States, the Coinage Act of 1965 states that the dollar is legal tender and must be accepted as repayment for all debts. This is the main reason we use dollars as monetary units.

4. *Unit of Account:* Money is the reference measure to set prices and to evaluate important economic indicators..

Kinds of Money

Through history, societies have used three kinds of money.

Commodity Money

In past centuries, people have used various commodities like gold and silver as money. Commodity money is inconvenient because it is heavy to carry, it is easy to debunk, and its value swings with changes in the demand and supply of the commodity.

Commodity-Backed Money

In more recent times, private and central banks started issuing paper certificates backed by gold that proved a more convenient means of payment. Under the **gold standard**, the dollar was backed by gold. At any time, the carrier of a dollar bill could visit the central bank and have the dollar bill converted into gold.

Fiat Money

Nowadays, most money is in the form of paper certificates that are not backed by gold or any other commodity. This is called **fiat money** because its value comes from people's trust that now and in the future the certificates will be accepted as a means of payment.

How Money Is Defined and Measured

The quantity of money in an economy is called the **money stock** or the **money supply**. Central banks use different definitions of the money stock. These are labeled with the capital letter M and a number. A lower number indicates a narrow definition of money that includes only very liquid assets.

Transaction deposits (for example, deposits in a checkable account) that can be withdrawn without limits are as liquid as cash and are considered money. Other forms of deposits that impose restrictions on withdrawals like NOW accounts, savings accounts, or time deposits are less liquid and are considered near money.

In the United States, the Federal Reserve Bank uses two monetary aggregates:

1. *M1*, which includes cash in circulation, checking accounts, and travelers' checks.
2. *M2*, which includes M1 and savings accounts, small time deposits, and retail money-market mutual funds.

TIP: An asset is liquid when it can be quickly and cheaply converted into cash. Assets that are highly liquid are also called near-money. The most liquid asset is cash itself.

Money and Other Assets

Money is a type of **financial asset**—an asset that derives value from a contractual claim. A **loan** is a type of financial asset that derives value from a contract that states that the borrower will pay money to the lender at some point in the future.

Another important class of financial assets is represented by **securities**. These are financial assets that can be traded. There are three classes of securities:

1. *Debt securities:* tradable *I Owe Yous*, like bank notes and bonds
2. *Equity securities:* standardized ownership shares like common stock
3. *Derivatives:* contracts where flows of money depend on the realization of uncertain events like futures, options, and swaps

Securities are traded in three types of markets: the primary market, the secondary market, and the open market. In the **primary market**, the issuer (the company that issues the security) sells the securities to the public and receives funds. In the **secondary market**, previously issued securities are exchanged between investors. Securities exchanged between the monetary authority (a.k.a. the central bank) and banks are traded in the **open market**.

Interest Rates

Unlike cash, other financial assets often pay interest. In a credit transaction, the money lent out at the start is called the **principal**, while the

interest is all the extra payments the lender receives from the borrower over the duration of the transaction. The **interest rate** is the ratio of interest to principal. Interest rates are measured in basis points. A **basis point** is one hundredth of one percent.

The interest rate is easy to compute in the case of a simple loan where a person lends M dollars to another and receives N dollars back at maturity. In this case, the interest is $I = (N - M)$ and the interest rate is $I = \dfrac{N - M}{M}$.

In the case of **fixed payment loans** (for example, a home mortgage loan or a coupon bond), computing the interest rate is more difficult. A common approach is to compute the yield to maturity. The **yield to maturity** is the interest rate that equates the current price of a debt security or loan to the present discounted value of all payments the lender will receive from the security or loan if he holds it until its maturity. The present discounted value of a future payment is the highest price at which you are willing to sell your claim to that payment.

There is a negative relationship between the price of a debt security, say a bond, and the interest rate. Bond prices increase when the demand for bonds increases and decline when the supply of bonds increases. Therefore, a higher demand for bonds leads to higher bond prices and lower interest rates; a higher supply of bonds leads to lower bond prices and higher interest rates. Debt securities can be more or less risky depending on the probability that the issuer might default, or not repay. Riskier securities are cheaper and pay a higher interest than safe securities. **Credit rating agencies** are firms that research the likelihood that different issuers might default and rate issuers' bonds accordingly.

TIP: Triple A ratings indicate no risk; C or D ratings indicate very high risk.

A **yield curve** is a graph that shows the interest rate on similar securities with different terms to maturity (the time remaining before the principal is repaid), for example, a three-month Treasury bill versus a 10-year Treasury bond. People are impatient—the interest rate on short-term securities (securities near maturity) is lower than the interest rate on long-term securities (securities far from maturity). Hence, the yield curve tends to be slightly upward sloping.

There is also a relationship between the slope of the yield curve and investors' expectations on the future behavior of short-term interest rates. If investors believe that short-term interest rates will soon rise, the yield curve becomes steeper. If investors believe that short-term interest rates will soon decline, the yield curve becomes flatter or even downward sloping.

COMMERCIAL BANKS AND OTHER FINANCIAL INTERMEDIARIES

Now that you have a better understanding of what money is, let's discuss **financial intermediaries**—institutions that move money from those who want to save it to those who want to borrow it.

Most financial intermediaries are depository institutions, normally called **banks**. Depository institutions are financial intermediaries that, by law, can accept deposits in transaction accounts and that together make up the banking sector.

In a nutshell, depository institutions accept funds from depositors and loan these funds out to families and businesses. A bank loan is called a **tool of indirect finance** as the bank intermediates between lenders (the depositors) and borrowers (loan applicants).

The banking sector of the United States has three distinguishing characteristics:

1. An unusually large number of small banks
2. A dual nature where some banks are chartered at the state level while others are nationally chartered
3. One of the most heavily regulated banking sectors in the world

The US banking sector was greatly shaped by the nation's history. American historical wariness for centralized power led to the unusually large number of small banks that still operate in the country, as, up until 1927, banks could be chartered only at the state level. Starting in 1927, with the passage of the **McFadden Act**, banks could be chartered at the national level. However, the Act subjected national banks to their home-state branching rules, effectively prohibiting interstate branching and severely limiting interstate banking. The limits on interstate banking were later lifted by the **Riegle-Neal Interstate Banking Act of 1994**, which relaxed branching rules and started an era of bank mergers.

The heavy regulatory environment typical of the US banking sector is a consequence of the duality of the system, as well as an inheritance of the stock market crash of 1929 and the wave of bank panics and bank failures that followed in the 1930s. In response to the financial upheaval, Congress passed the Banking Act of 1933, often called the **Glass-Steagall Act**, which imposed limitations on the type of activities that banks could engage in and on the interest rates they could pay on deposit accounts.

Also, since the banking sector is dual, most banks are regulated both at the state and at the national level, and they are subject to supervision from state and federal agencies. Starting in the 1980s, the US banking sector witnessed a process of deregulation. In 1980, the **Depository Institutions Deregulation and Monetary Control Act (DIDMCA)** allowed banks to pay interest on special demand deposits called NOW accounts. Starting from the mid 1990s, the reinterpretation and then complete repeal of the Glass-Steagall Act (Gramm-Leach-Bliley Act of 1999) allowed banks to engage in a wide array of nonbank financial activities.

Structure of the US Banking Industry

In the United States, there are three types of depository institutions: **commercial banks**, **thrifts**, and **credit unions**.

Commercial Banks

Commercial banks are the largest category of financial intermediaries by value of assets. In the United States, commercial banks can be chartered and supervised by states (state banks) or by the Office of the Comptroller of the Currency (OCC), a branch of the Federal Treasury (national banks). All national banks and some state banks are members of the **Federal Reserve System**.

Most commercial banks have assets between $100 million and $500 million. However, the largest commercial banks have assets of more than $10 billion each, which means the largest 1 percent of banks holds more than 70 percent of all banking assets. Commercial banks are stock owned and earn profit by accepting deposits, extending loans, investing in securities, and offering various financial services for a fee. Deposits at commercial banks are insured by the **Federal Deposit Insurance Corporation (FDIC)** for up to $250,000 per account.

TIP: While the number of commercial banks has steadily declined in the past few decades, the number of bank branches has increased twofold since the early 1970s—banks realized that proximity to home or the workplace was a key factor in people's decision about where to bank.

"Thrifts": Savings Associations and Savings and Loans Associations (S&Ls)

More than 1,000 US banks are Saving Associations (SAs) and Savings and Loans Associations (S&Ls). These primarily extend residential loans. They started as mutual institutions that collected members' funds through savings (thrift) deposits and financed residential developments for their members. Nowadays, many such associations are stock owned, accept demand deposits, and extend a wider variety of loans.

SAs and S&Ls can be chartered at the state or national level and are regulated by the Office of Thrift Supervision (OTS), which is now merged with the OCC. Deposits at SAs and S&Ls are insured by the FDIC. In the 1980s, a spike in interest rates led to a severe crisis of the S&Ls system, which was then overhauled. Nowadays, thanks to a number of regulatory changes, S&Ls perform many of the same activities as commercial banks.

Credit Unions

Credit unions are mutual institutions where members with a common bond deposit saving shares and apply for consumer loans. Because of the common bond, these institutions are quite small and, like other types of clubs, benefit from tax advantages and are not subject to antitrust regulation. They can be chartered by states or at the national level. The National Credit Union Administration regulates and oversees federally chartered credit unions and the National Credit Union Share Insurance Fund (NCU-SIF) insures deposits at all credit unions for up to $250,000 per account. In time of crisis, credit unions can borrow funds from the Central Liquidity Facility (CLF).

Other Financial Intermediaries

Banks are just one type of financial intermediary. Several other types of firms offer different services of financial intermediation. With the deregulation of the banking sector, today's bank holding companies are often made up of various financial intermediaries.

The other most important types of financial companies are:

- **Investment banks:** Investment banks help companies issue securities like stocks and bonds to raise funds directly from the public (unlike commercial banks that offer borrowers indirect finance). They also assist companies with mergers and acquisitions and risk management.

- **Insurance companies:** Insurance companies are financial intermediaries that help people better manage the risks in their lives and protect themselves from financial losses. Typically, insurance companies offer contracts in which, for the payment of a fixed premium, they promise to reimburse certain expenses, such as medical expenses or car repairs after an accident.
- **Mutual funds/pensions funds:** Mutual funds are professionally managed pools of funds invested in various securities like stocks and bonds. The funds' owners are called shareholders. Funds that are used to pay pensions are called **pension funds**.
- **Bank Holding Company (BHC):** These are financial companies that own one or more banks.

In the past couple of decades, the importance of these financial intermediaries has significantly grown. They often lend funds just like commercial banks would do; however, instead of doing so by extending loans, they channel funds through the various securities markets. Often, these institutions are referred to as the **shadow banking system**.

Operation and Management of Financial Markets and Intermediaries

Commercial banks and other financial intermediaries are for-profit enterprises. Banks earn profit by charging fees (credit card fees, for example) and by borrowing funds at a low interest rate and lending those funds at a higher interest rate. Economists call this activity **asset transformation**.

Here is an example of asset transformation. When an individual deposits $1,000 in a checkable account at ABC Bank, the deposit increases the ABC Bank's reserves by $1,000. By law, the bank must keep a share of the deposit as required reserves. (In the United States, the required reserve ratio varies depending on the size of the bank, with higher ratios imposed on larger banks.) However, the bank can loan out up to the full amount of its excess reserves.

Suppose the required reserve ratio is 10 percent. After a deposit of $1,000, ABC Bank can loan out up to $1,000 – (10% × $1,000) = $900. If ABC Bank pays an interest rate of 0.5% on its checkable deposit and charges an interest rate of 5% on its loans, at the end of the year, the Bank has (5% × $900) – (0.5% × $1,000) = $45 – $5 = $40 of income it can use to pay for nonfinancial expenses and to distribute a dividend to its stockholders.

The Balance Sheet of a Commercial Bank

To fully understand the different activities performed by financial interme-diaries, it is important to understand how these organizations raise funds and use them. We can do so in an organized way by taking a quick look at the typical balance sheet of a commercial bank.

The **balance sheet** is an accounting tool with two columns, one listing a firm's **liabilities** (money owed) and **capital** (net worth) and the other list-ing the firm's **assets**. At all times, the two sides balance:

assets = liabilities + capital

A bank's liabilities and capital show how the bank raises money, while the bank's assets show how the bank uses that money.

Liabilities

Liabilities are funds the bank owes to some person or business. The larger share of a commercial bank's liabilities is in the form of deposits. These come in three types:

1. *Demand deposits:* Deposits that can be withdrawn without limits like check-able accounts (18 percent of all deposits). Until 2011, they were not allowed to pay interest in accordance with Regulation Q, the regulation that in accor-dance with the Banking Act of 1933 (Glass-Steagall Act) prohibited paying interest on deposits payable on demand.
   - Negotiable Orders of Withdrawal (NOW) accounts: Introduced by the DIDMCA in 1980, these are deposits that, while structured similarly to checking accounts, were not considered demand deposits and hence were allowed to pay interest in compliance with Regulation Q.
2. *Savings deposits* (61 percent of all deposits) There are two main types of saving deposits:
   - *Savings accounts:* Accounts that pay interest but that do not allow writ-ing checks (20 percent)
   - *Money market deposit accounts:* Similar to money market mutual funds shares; however, they are federally insured and pay interest. The law limits transfers to third parties to six per month (47 percent).
3. *Time deposits:* (15 percent of all deposits) The funds in time deposits are available only at a specified time in the future (maturity date). The two most important types of time deposits are:
   - *Certificates of Deposit (CDs):* Certificates issued in specific amounts that pay a fixed-interest rate.

- *Negotiable Certificates of Deposit:* These have larger denominations than regular CDs ($100,000 or more) and are negotiable.

Other important liabilities on a commercial bank's balance sheets are:

- **Borrowed funds:** Funds borrowed from wholesale money markets. Their importance increased as demand for loans outpaced banks' ability to attract new deposits.
- **Federal funds:** Funds held at the Federal Reserve as required or excess reserves.
- **Repurchase agreements (repos):** A form of loan where the bank sells a security to a lender with the promise to repurchase the same security for a specified price at a specified date.
- **Eurodollars:** These are deposits denominated in dollars but held in foreign branches of US banks (or at foreign banks). The interest rate banks charge each other in the Eurodollar market is called the London Interbank Offer Rate (LIBOR).
- **Fed loans:** These are funds the bank has borrowed from the discount window of the Federal Reserve. The term is typically 15 days.
- **Trading liabilities:** Funds owed due to losses on derivative contracts or due to short positions (when the bank sells securities it does not own).

Bank Capital

A bank's equity capital is also called **net worth**. Banks have lower capital than most other firms. The smaller the ratio of a bank's capital to its assets, the more leveraged the bank is. There are two types of bank capital:

1. *Capital stock:* The funds stockholders have directly invested in the bank
2. *Undivided profits:* Profit that has not yet been paid out as dividend

Assets

Under assets, we find the different uses of the deposited or borrowed funds. The majority of assets comes from money that others owe to the bank. Here are some of the main examples of assets:

- **Cash assets:** Very liquid assets the bank holds as cash in vault or funds deposited at the Federal Reserve Bank
- **Fed funds sold and reverse repos:** The reverse of a repurchase; in this case, the bank is lending funds by purchasing securities from the borrower, who agrees to repurchase them at a future date for a specified price

- **Investments:** Highly liquid portfolios of bonds issued by the US government or a US government agency or a municipality; they can be easily sold when the bank is in need of reserves, and they give tax benefits. Bonds are standardized contracts that provide the issuer financing but no other service
- **Loans:** More than 55 percent of commercial banks' assets are represented by loans; loans are not as liquid as investment assets and are contracts specifically designed to address each customer's needs. Most bank loans are secured with some form of collateral. If the lender defaults on the loan, the bank acquires ownership of the collateral. A mortgage, for example, is a secured (or collateralized) loan. Some loans charge a fixed interest rate, while others charge a floating interest rate that moves following a benchmark rate (like the LIBOR or the prime rate). Banks extend commercial loans to businesses, real estate loans (mortgages) to individuals and businesses for the purchase or remodeling of buildings and structures, agricultural loans to farmers, and consumer loans to individuals. Bank credit cards are a growing type of consumer loan. The first credit cards offered only local credit, but, starting in 1966 with changes in bank regulations, they have become a national phenomenon. A cardholder has access to funds up to a set limit and each billing cycle must pay a minimum installment. Interest is charged on any purchase not covered within the monthly billing cycle.
- **Leases:** Starting in the mid 60s, banks could purchase items that they lease to individuals or businesses; this type of contract has tax advantages.

Key Management Activities

Let's have a closer look at these important facets of bank management.

Liquidity Management

When a bank has to meet an unusually high volume of withdrawals, it can generate the necessary reserves in several ways. The bank could borrow funds in the federal funds market, sell some liquid securities, borrow funds from the Federal Reserve through the discount window, or reduce the stock of loans—either by not renewing some of the short-term loans that reach maturity that day (that is, by calling in loans) or by selling some loans to other financial intermediaries.

Each of these actions comes at a different opportunity cost. For example, the bank has to pay the federal funds rate on funds borrowed in the federal funds market and the discount rate on funds borrowed from the Federal Reserve. Calling in loans can spoil the relationship with a valuable client.

The bank manager has to decide which option is the most profitable and in the end might decide that the bank should hold a large volume of excess reserves instead.

Asset Management

Bank managers purchase and sell assets and liabilities to reach three goals: earn the highest returns, avoid risk, and guarantee liquidity. There are four strategies bank managers can follow to reach their goals. They can seek borrowers who are willing to pay high interest even if they have a limited risk of default, they can buy securities that pay high returns even if their risk is low, they can diversify the bank portfolio, and they can hold some very liquid securities even if these pay low interest.

Liability Management

After the 1960s, checkable deposits ceased to be the main source of funds at commercial banks. Now, when a commercial bank wants to raise funds, it can sell a negotiable CD or borrow funds in the federal funds market. Banks can increase their profit by paying attention to the composition of their liabilities.

Capital Adequacy Management

Banks face a tradeoff when choosing an adequate level of bank capital. On the one hand, banks must keep a minimum amount of capital to avoid failure and to meet regulatory requirements. On the other hand, the capital stock affects the rate of return the bank can pay to its investors. Economists use two measures to assess a bank's profitability:

The Return on Average Assets (ROAA):

$$\text{ROAA} = \frac{\text{Net income (i.e., returns after taxes)}}{\text{Assets}}$$

The Return on Average Equity (ROAE):

$$\text{ROAE} = \frac{\text{Net income (i.e., returns after taxes)}}{\text{Equity Capital}}$$

For a given return on assets, the lower the capital stock, the higher the return on average equity.

Risk Management

Banks face two sources of risk that could rock their operations and push them in the red: credit risk and interest-rate risk. **Credit risk** refers to the possibility that borrowers default on their loans, while **interest-rate risk** refers to the possibility of sudden changes in the interest rate the bank charges its debtors or pays to its creditors.

Managing Credit Risk

Information asymmetries on borrowers' creditworthiness lead to a problem called **adverse selection**, where charging higher interest rates attracts riskier borrowers—in effect, selecting an adverse outcome for the bank. Information asymmetries on borrowers' choices and actions lead to a problem called **moral hazard**, in which, since banks cannot monitor borrowers' use of funds, borrowers have an incentive to take up more risk than they can handle, consequently raising the hazard of default.

There are several strategies bank managers can follow to reduce moral hazard and adverse selection:

- They can collect detailed information on loan applicants, screening out borrowers with higher chances of default.
- They can visit commercial borrowers to monitor how they are employing the borrowed funds.
- They can specialize in specific types of loans or in specific geographical areas to gain higher expertise and reduce the cost of screening and monitoring.

The tool banks most commonly use to reduce moral hazard is collateral requirements. **Collateral** is any asset that by contract the bank acquires in case of default. Vehicles, real estate, or financial assets are used often as collateral. **Compensating balances**, funds the borrower must keep deposited at the lending bank for the duration of the loan, are another form of collateral.

To limit moral hazard, banks develop long-term bank relationships with their clients, who then find it more costly to choose projects that raise their risk of default on a loan. Long-term relationships also lower the cost of screening and monitoring future loan applications from the same client. Adverse selection and moral hazard can lead banks to ration credit by either refusing to lend any amount of funds to some borrowers or by limiting the amount of funds a borrower can obtain at the offered interest rate.

Managing Interest-Rate Risk

Interest-rate volatility raises a bank's earnings volatility, exposing the bank to undesired risk. There are two approaches economists use to analyze interest rate risk: **gap analysis**, which focuses on the difference between interest rate-sensitive liabilities and interest rate-sensitive assets, and **duration analysis**, which evaluates how changes in interest rates affect the value of assets and liabilities in the bank's balance sheet. The name of this approach comes from the relationship between a security's market value, the interest rate, and the number of years during which the security will produce a stream of payments, called the security's **duration**.

> **TIP:** Banks also earn income (or incur losses) on trades of derivative securities like forwards, futures, and swaps.

Off-Balance Sheet Banking

As banks have become more reliant on fee-based activities instead of interest-based activities, a larger share of banks' activities are not reflected in changes of the balance sheet. These are the so-called off-balance sheet activities. Banks charge fees on a variety of financial services from foreign exchange trades to the creation of structured investment vehicles and securitization.

More traditional off-balance sheet activities, however, are loan commitments, promises to lend money according to agreed rules. Credit card limits, lines of credit, and revolving credit are three kinds of loan commitments. Banks are also more likely to engage in loan sales and loan brokerage. If they have specific expertise in a geographic area or a type of client, banks earn profit by cheaply originating loans they resell at a higher price to other financial intermediaries. The practice has become so widespread that the loan-related data in call reports are becoming less and less informative of the overall volume of loan origination.

Regulation of the Banking Industry

Governments that wish to mitigate adverse selection and moral hazard in credit markets heavily regulate the banking sector to protect consumers from abuses and to enhance the stability of the financial system.

As we mentioned earlier, in the United States, several agencies charter, regulate, and supervise commercial banks and other depository institutions, and it is possible for the same financial institution to be regulated and supervised by up to four different state or federal agencies.

Banking regulation and supervision is very complex. The following sections will break it down into its most relevant categories.

Capital Requirements

Capital requirements are regulations that force banks to keep a sound amount of capital. Banks with more capital are less likely to fail.

Equity capital is an effective buffer when a bank must absorb losses. Also, more capital means the bank has more to lose from poor management and risky activities significantly reducing problems of moral hazard. Until the mid 1980s, capital requirements were set in terms of the leverage ratio, the ratio between core capital and total assets. In 1988, however, the central bankers of the United States and eleven other high-income countries signed an accord known as Basel 1 that introduced the idea of tying capital requirements to a bank's risk exposure.

In the United States, current regulation now divides capital in two categories, called **Tier 1 capital** (or core capital) and **Tier 2 capital** (or supplemental capital) and requires a bank's leverage ratio be higher than 3 percent and that the ratio of Tier 1 plus Tier 2 capital to risk-weighted assets be at least 8 percent. When computing risk-weighted assets, assets are divided into four categories from less risky to more risky and assigned different weights. Off-balance sheet activities are also factored in after they are converted into on-balance sheet equivalents and assigned to the different risk categories.

Implementation of the original Basel accord highlighted how banks can increase their effective risk exposure without affecting their measured exposure by holding riskier assets within each asset category, an activity economists call **regulatory arbitrage**. The guidelines of the original Basel accord were revised in 1999 to strengthen the link between capital requirements and risk for large international banks. However, the suggested capital requirements proved too low to protect large banks from the financial crisis of 2008.

Financial Supervision and Bank Examinations

To protect the public from scams, banks are chartered after a long review process. Charter applicants must provide extensive information on the bank's business plan, suggested senior management, and financial viability. Once operating, banks must file quarterly call reports describing the bank's operations and financial conditions. Banks are also subject to periodic unannounced safety and soundness examinations. Bank examiners review the bank's records for possible fraud, analyze assets (loans in particular) and liabilities to assess the bank's creditworthiness, and verify management's ability to identify and monitor risk. Regulators use information from the call reports and the on-site examinations to rate each bank on a scale from 1 (highest) to 5 (lowest) according to the **CAMELS rating system**, which stands for **C**apital, **A**sset quality, **M**anagement, **E**arnings, **L**iquidity, and **S**ensitivity to market risk. Starting in the mid 90s, regulators raised their emphasis on supervising banks' risk management, and large banks must pass **stress tests**, simulations that assess how the bank would weather severe economic shocks and whether the bank needs to raise more capital.

Disclosure Requirements

To alleviate problems of asymmetric information, regulators require banks to disclose information on the composition of their assets and risk exposure. Disclosure requirements allow investors, stockholders, and depositors to gain all the information they need about the financial condition of a bank to make good decisions. Indirectly, this nudges bank managers to steer away from excessively risky activities. Disclosure requirements were first introduced in the 1930s and were greatly tightened by the Sarbanes-Oxley Act of 2002.

Consumer Protection

Another goal of bank regulation and supervision is to protect consumers from scams, discrimination, and predatory lending practices. Starting in 1969, the Truth in Lending Act (Consumer Credit Protection Act, CCPA) requires that lenders (including banks) give borrowers clear and correct information on the interest rate they pay. For each loan, creditors must clearly indicate the **annual percentage rate (APR)** and total finance charges. The Fair Credit Billing Act (FCBA) requires that credit card issuers clearly state how they will assess finance charges and that they resolve billing disputes quickly. The Fair and Accurate Credit Transaction (FACT) act regulates credit-reporting agencies, protecting them from state-level over-regulation and requiring that each year consumers are entitled to a free credit report.

The Equal Credit Opportunity Act (ECOA) forbids banks from discriminating according to race, age, gender, marital status, and national origin, while the Community Reinvestment Act (CRA) of 1977 requires that banks offer credit to individuals and firms from all neighborhoods in their market area and refrain from **redlining**, the practice of using a red marker to highlight on a map neighborhoods where the bank does not extend loans.

Compliance with the CRA regulation is heavy in documentation and costly. What's worse, by requiring banks to offer loans in all areas, including economically depressed neighborhoods, the CRA has the unintended consequence of leading banks to extend risky loans to financially weak families that are unable to repay and end up bankrupt.

Deposit Insurance

In this section, we will explore the regulations and the agency that help keep the banking sector stable and stop bank failures from becoming bank panics.

Bank Failures and Lender of Last Resort

As we mentioned earlier, when a bank can no longer meet its obligations to depositors and creditors, it fails. A bank failure can be triggered by **illiquidity** or **insolvency**. During a bank crisis, depositors withdraw their funds all at once, and even a sound bank can find itself illiquid and unable to meet its obligations. In such a time, even sound banks are forced to sell security investments at a loss, losing assets and risking bankruptcy. Central banks prevent this type of failure by acting as **lenders of last resort**. Since 1914, the Federal Reserve offers liquidity to distressed member banks through its discount window or through open market operations, acting as a lender of last resort to these intermediaries.

Excessive risk-taking lies behind failures triggered by **insolvency**. As we mentioned before, bank managers tend to extend loans and buy securities that are risky, as these pay higher interest. However, if creditors default on their loans and security prices drop, the bank can suddenly lose assets and, unless it has an adequate amount of equity capital, it quickly finds itself unable to repay short-term debt or meet depositors' cash withdrawals. Capital requirements help prevent failures due to insolvency.

Before new regulation was introduced in the 1930s, bank failures spread like a contagious disease. If a single bank failed, depositors became nervous due to the asymmetric nature of information. Since they could not tell if their bank was sound or on the brink of collapse, wary customers rushed to withdraw funds at the same time, triggering bank runs and bank panics. Economists call this phenomenon the **financial contagion effect**.

The Federal Deposit Insurance Corporation

From the late 1800s through the 1930s, bank failures were a serious problem, and bank panics were frequent. Between 1920 and 1933, more than 10,000 banks failed. By statute, only member banks could borrow from the Federal Reserve as lender of last resort, and fewer than 10 percent of depository institutions were members. The number of bank failures, however, dropped precipitously after the establishment of the **Federal Deposit Insurance Corporation (FDIC)** by the Glass-Steagall Act in 1933.

The FDIC insures deposit accounts and prevents bank runs and panics very effectively. Today, the FDIC insures depositors at commercial banks and S&L associations for up to $250,000 per account. The National Credit Union Share Insurance Fund insures accounts at credit unions. While all types of deposit accounts (checking accounts, savings accounts, money market accounts, and certificates of deposit) are insured, the FDIC does not cover other financial products, like investment accounts, shares in mutual funds, or life insurance.

Let's discuss how the FDIC handles failed banks. Typically, insolvent banks are shut down by their chartering authority; in rare cases, however, after a negative examination, the FDIC makes the decision to resolve a failing bank. Once the decision to shut down a bank has been made, there are two methods the FDIC can use to resolve the failed business: the payoff and liquidate method and the purchase and assumption method. By law, the FDIC must use the method with lowest cost.

Under the **payoff and liquidate method**, the FDIC pays off depositors up to $250,000 per account, and then liquidates all the bank's assets to pay off all other debts. Creditors have different levels of precedence: depositors and the FDIC are paid off first, then general creditors, and last, if any money is left, it pays shareholders. Under the **purchase and assumption method**, the FDIC brokers the sale or merger of the failing bank with a willing and financially stable institution. The FDIC often facilitates the deal by extending subsidized loans or by assuming some of the bad loans and investments of the failing bank. Under a **clean bank purchase and assumption**, the assuming bank keeps only the failing bank's insured deposits and purchases only few of the bank's assets. On the other hand, under a **whole bank agreement**, the assuming bank receives all assets and liabilities for a one-time payment.

Deposit Insurance and Moral Hazard

Deposit insurance reduces the risk of financial contagion and the likelihood of bank panics; however, it creates several types of moral hazard. Deposit insurance reduces depositors' need to monitor their banks worsening market discipline. Because insured depositors do not bear any of the bank's risk, managers are able to attract deposits at low interest even while extending risky loans. Even if these loans fail, the bank can still look profitable by propping up earnings with origination fees, since it can still attract cheap deposits to raise loanable funds.

Too Big to Fail (TBTF)

The FDIC has always shied away from liquidating large failing banks, creating an incentive for shareholders, uninsured depositors, and creditors to own or do business with large banks instead of smaller banks.

In 1984, when one of the largest American banks called Continental Illinois almost failed, the FDIC went a step further and announced that a number of very large American banks were "too big to fail" and would never be liquidated. The policy wanted to prevent instability in the banking sector. One bank's liability is another bank's asset, and the liquidation of one very large bank could drastically reduce the value of other banks' assets, triggering bank runs and bank panic. However, the too big to fail policy exacerbates the problems of moral hazard we mentioned earlier, and it gives large banks an unfair advantage in attracting depositors at low interest rates, as all deposits at TBTF banks are effectively insured.

However, in September 2008, the failure of Lehman Brothers, an investment bank, had dramatic consequences on the financial system, highlighting that indeed some financial institutions are too big to fail and heightening regulators' emphasis on what economists call **systemic risk**—events that would rock the whole banking and financial system instead of just one financial intermediary.

MONEY AND MACROECONOMIC ACTIVITY

In this section, we'll outline different theories that explain how the economy works and how money supply and interest rates influence economic activity and our everyday lives. This knowledge will help you better understand when and how central banks can influence inflation and employment with their tools of monetary policy.

Basic Classical and Keynesian Economics

Before diving into the theories, let's review some common economic terminology.

Economists call **total output** the amount of goods and services an economy produces in a year, and they track total output using an economic indicator called **Gross Domestic Product (GDP). Potential output** is the level of output the economy produces when inputs, labor in particular, are fully employed and the economy operates efficiently.

Gross domestic product is the value of all final goods and services produced for the market over a period of time in the country. A **final good** is an item that is not used and totally transformed in production over the same period. GDP has four components: **consumption**, **investment**, **government spending**, and **net exports** (the difference between exports to other nations and imports from other nations). Consumption counts families' expenditures in durable and nondurable goods. Investment has two components: **fixed investment**, which counts expenditures on residential and nonresidential structures and firms' purchases of new equipment and machinery, and **inventory expenditure**, which counts changes in firms' holdings of materials, parts, and final products.

The payment people receive for their work or financial investment is called **income**. Economists track income using the economic indicator **net national income (NNI)**. Net national income has four components: wages and salaries, rents, interest, and profit.

Economists call **disposable income (DI)** the difference of **net national income** and **net taxes**. Every year, families pay a portion of their income in taxes and receive a portion of their income as transfers from government social security pension. Net taxes are the difference between taxes and transfers.

Families spend a portion of their **disposable income** (after-taxes income) in consumption (just like the GDP component) and the save the rest. Hence, disposable income is the sum of consumption and saving.

The **price level** is an average of all prices and is tracked using several indicators, for example the Consumer Price Index (CPI) or the Personal Consumption Expenditures (PCE) deflator.

Inflation is a continual and generalized increase in the price level. The inflation rate measures how fast prices are increasing.

Unemployment is the number of jobless workers in search of work. **Employment** is the number of workers who have jobs. The **unemployment rate** is the ratio of unemployment to the labor force, the sum of unemployment and employment. When people are out of work because they don't have skills in demand, they are deemed *structurally unemployed*. When people are out of work due to a low level of economic activity, they are deemed *cyclically unemployed*. The economy is called at full employment when there is no cyclical unemployment.

The **interest rate** is the proportion of a loan or of the value of a debt security that is charged as interest. The **real interest rate** is the difference between the interest rate and the rate of inflation people feel will prevail in the future.

TIP: All these relationships can be summarized in the following way: GDP ≈ NNI and NNI = Net Taxes = Disposable Income = Consumption + Saving

---

Theories

This section focuses on two economic approaches: the classical approach and the Keynesian approach (after British economist John Maynard Keynes).

Classical economists believe the economy is self-regulating and advocate for a **laissez-faire** (let it be) approach to economic policy. According to the classical model, total output follows the amount of labor input and capital input used in production. These amounts are determined in highly competitive markets where flexible prices absorb any change in demand or supply.

In the labor market, workers' and firms' decisions are driven by the **real wage**, the amount of goods the monetary wage can buy. The **supply of labor** is an upward sloping line illustrating that at higher wages, more people are willing to work. The **demand for labor** is a downward sloping line illustrating that at higher wages, firms have lower profit margins and hire fewer workers. The market is in **equilibrium** when firms pay the wage rate where the demand for labor is equal to the supply of labor. Flexible real wages that move in response to changes in demand and supply maintain the market in equilibrium at all times; when the labor market is in equilibrium, all people willing to accept the current wage have found a job, and the only people out of work are those who don't wish to work for the current wage. There is no involuntary unemployment.

The key idea of the classical model is that the market for goods and services is in equilibrium at all times because *supply creates its own demand*, a statement that is often referred to as **Say's law**. Classical economists noted that for every $10 of output a firm produces, $10 of income is paid to workers and entrepreneurs. If in one way or another all of this income is spent to buy goods and services, the very act of producing an item creates the demand for that item.

In the classical model, the market for capital makes sure savings would equate investment, so all income distributed would come back to firms in the form of demand—some as consumption and some as investment. In the classical model's view, in the market for capital families loan out funds to firms that wish to finance their investment spending.

Families and firms base their saving and investment decisions primarily on the real interest rate. The supply of funds is upward sloping, as families are more willing to postpone consumption and save when the interest rate is higher. The demand for funds is downward sloping, as a decline in the interest rate lowers borrowing costs and increases the number of investment projects that are profitable. In equilibrium, the demand for loanable funds equals the supply of loanable funds and investment equates saving.

TIP: Early economists believed flexible interest rates adjusted to movements of demand and supply and maintained investment equal to saving and the demand for goods and services equal to the supply of goods and services at all times.

Keynesian economists believe the economy fails to self-adjust at times and that economic policy—in particular, higher government spending—can help maintain the economy at full employment.

According to these economists, prices and wages are sticky and total output follows aggregate expenditures. **Aggregate expenditures** are the sum of four components: consumption, planned investment, government purchases, and net exports.

- **Consumption expenditure** is the largest of the four components and, according to the Keynesian model, it's positively related to current disposable income. Consumption sensitivity to disposable income is called the Marginal Propensity to Consume (MPC): C = Autonomous consumption + MPC × Disposable Income.
- **Planned investment** is the sum of planned fixed investment and planned inventory investment. Keynes agreed with the classical economists that it is negatively sensitive to changes in the cost of borrowing and the real interest rate: I = autonomous investment – d × real interest rate.
- **Government purchases** add directly to total spending, while taxes reduce total spending indirectly reducing disposable income and lowering consumption.
- **Net exports** are sensitive to changes in the foreign exchange rate, to the relative price of domestic and foreign goods and to global economic conditions. A higher interest rate influences the foreign exchange rate and leads to an appreciation of the domestic currency. As a result, net exports are negatively sensitive to the interest rate.

In the Keynesian model, the market for goods and services can be in equilibrium with the economy operating below its potential level and workers being involuntarily out of jobs. Also, since consumption is sensitive to disposable income, changes in aggregate expenditure are amplified by a **multiplier effect.**

According to Keynesian economists, a decline in investment lowers aggregate expenditure and increases inventory investment above its planned level. Firms that see their finite product pile up in their warehouses cut production and let some workers go. As prices and wages are sticky, the real wage does not decline when labor demand drops, and unemployment rises as the economy slows down. Many workers out of jobs are involuntarily unemployed at the current monetary wage at which they would accept work. In modern terminology, they are cyclically unemployed since weak spending is behind their joblessness.

Keynesian economists believed that public policy is effective at stimulating the economy during a recession or cooling it off during inflationary times. Because the banking sector was weak and in upheaval when Keynes wrote most of his theory in the 1930s, early Keynesians tended to favor fiscal policy (in the form of actions taken by the central government like higher public spending) as particularly effective at supporting the economy in times of depression. Keynesian economists pointed out that higher government purchases would increase total spending, creating demand for private businesses and triggering a positive income/consumption multiplier effect.

Classical economists, on the contrary, believed fiscal policy could never stimulate the economy. Classical economists stressed that higher government spending must be financed either by higher taxes today or by higher taxes in the future; and that in both cases, families anticipating the tax hike would lower consumption, neutralizing the positive effects of the fiscal policy.

After WWII, Keynesian economists believed that the government could run public deficits during economic downturns and surpluses during expansions to fine tune the economy, that is, to preempt possible swings in economic activity. They also thought that the central bank could stimulate the economy with little consequence for the inflation rate. A study of empirical data had found a negative relationship between the inflation rate and the unemployment rate, called the **Phillips curve**, and some Keynesian economists believed this relationship to be structural and immutable, providing the central bank with a policy trade-off.

Monetarism and Rational Expectations

During the 1960s and 1970s, however, the yearly inflation rate increased from 1.2 percent in 1964 to 11.8 percent in 1974, and economists' focus shifted from maintaining the economy at full employment to understanding and fighting inflation. It is in these years that a new theory called **monetarism** came to the fore.

Monetarists believed that fiscal policy is ineffective at stimulating the economy and that monetary policy can affect economic activity in the short run, while it affects only prices and inflation in the long run. These economists believed that due to long policy lags, monetary policy would disrupt the economy instead of stabilize it and suggested a fixed rate of growth of the money supply as the optimal policy.

Monetarists believed that inflation is always a monetary phenomenon and stressed the importance of expectations during inflationary times. Milton Friedman, the most prominent of the monetarists, pointed out that the inflation/unemployment trade-off, or the Phillips curve, was not stable, but shifted up along the inflation dimension as people adjusted their inflation expectations. Friedman believed that people had adaptive expectations and would adjust their inflation expectations rather slowly.

In the early '80s, a new group of economists stressed that not only did inflation expectations adjust rather quickly, but also that people used all their knowledge of the economy and the monetary policy when forming expectations. They believed that people have rational expectations; they thought that the economy works the way people expect and that people form expectations using all available information without making systematic mistakes. If people have rational expectations, monetary policy is neutral also in the short run.

Money and Inflation

Economists have shown that a faster money supply can lead to inflation. There are three theories of inflation.

The Quantity Theory of Inflation

The quantity theory of inflation states that a higher rate of growth of the money supply leads to faster inflation. At the heart of this theory is the **equation of exchange** that states that income at current prices is equal to the money supply times the velocity of money: $P \times Y = M \times V$. The velocity of money is the number of times that each dollar note must change hands over the year so that all transactions are paid for.

The quantity theory of inflation makes the assumption that the velocity of money does not change through time and that the economy is always at potential output, so that changes in the money supply M translate into changes in the level of prices P—in other words, inflation.

Demand-Pull Inflation

The demand-pull inflation theory is a more sophisticated version of the quantity theory of inflation. In this theory, it is recognized that higher money supply lowers interest rates and stimulates investment and consumption, raising total spending. If total spending increases faster than total output, however, the result is a continual increase in the price level, in other words inflation. Many economists believe that the increasing inflation of the 1960s and 1970s was an example of demand-pull inflation.

Cost-Push Inflation

Inflation could also arise from increases in the cost of production. This is what economists call cost-push inflation. For example, a sudden increase in the cost of imported materials like petroleum or copper would force firms to raise their prices and could trigger a wage/price spiral where workers demand higher wages to protect their purchasing power and firms agree to the wage increases just to increase prices even further.

CENTRAL BANKING AND THE FEDERAL RESERVE SYSTEM

The central bank of the United States is called the Federal Reserve System. A central bank is the institution that supervises a nation's banking sector and is in charge of the money supply.

TIP: Before 1913, the United States had no central bank.

Historical and Philosophical Framework

The Federal Reserve System was created in 1913, when Congress passed the **Federal Reserve Act**.

In the early years of the Union, at the urgency of Alexander Hamilton, who believed a national bank could improve credit conditions and spur economic development, Congress established a First Bank of the United States as a repository of federal funds. However, in 1811, the bank's charter was allowed to expire. The second attempt at creating a central bank failed in 1836. The predominantly agrarian society of the early Union, represented by Andrew Jackson, was wary of concentrated power and feared that a central bank would represent only the interests of bankers and industrialists.

Between 1836 and 1865, the so-called **free banking era**, the United States had thousands of state chartered banks that extended loans funded via the issuance of bank notes. The country had no centralized currency and people used these thousands of different bank notes as money. Each bank's note carried the issuer's risk of failure and notes issued by well-run banks were exchanged at their face value, while notes issued by poorly managed banks were exchanged at a discount.

During the years of the Civil War, Congress passed the **National Bank Acts**, which led to the current dual nature of the US banking system. The

Acts empowered the Comptroller of the Currency to charter national banks that could issue tax-exempt national notes backed by government securities. State bank notes were subject to a 10 percent tax and the Act reduced the number of currencies in circulation but increased state banks' reliance on demand deposits as their main source of liquidity. Demand deposits were not insured, and state banks kept scant reserves, often reinvested at other depository institutions; as a result, bank runs and bank panics were very frequent. At the time, most banks extended call loans, loans that borrowers had to repay the moment the bank needed the money back.

During panics, banks in dire need of liquidity would call their loans in, pushing cash strapped farmers and businesses into bankruptcy and plunging entire regions into deep economic depressions. The worst of these came in 1907 when a severe financial crisis in the New York Stock Exchange spread to the banking sector and then engulfed the whole economy. The joint intervention of some of the richest men in America saved the economy, but time was ripe for the creation of a central bank to bring some stability to the US financial system.

Between 1908 and 1912, a national monetary commission chaired by Senator Nelson Aldrich worked at the design of a decentralized, banker-controlled monetary authority. However, in 1912, the newly elected Woodrow Wilson abandoned Aldrich's proposal and instructed Carter Glass and Parker Willis to craft an alternative plan for a government-controlled central bank. With several compromises on the way, Glass' and Willis' proposal evolved into the Federal Reserve Act of 1913.

The Act established a central bank that would bring stability to the financial system, streamline check collection and clearing, and provide strong supervision to the banking sector. The bank was authorized to issue Federal Reserve notes convertible into gold that it would use to maintain an "elastic currency" accommodating businesses' needs for liquidity as prescribed by the real bills doctrine. Reflecting the current fears of concentration of power, the Reserve System was organized in twelve regional districts, each with a Federal Bank owned by local member banks.

Surprisingly, even if the Federal Reserve's main mandate was preserving financial stability, the Federal Reserve Bank was not given the full authority to act as a lender of last resort; the Bank could lend to institutions in financial distress only if they were member banks, and these were always a minority of all depository institutions.

Structure and Organization

The structure and organization of the Federal Reserve System clearly reflects the institution's history and a clear desire for compromise between stability and decentralization.

The Federal Reserve System is composed of a Board of Governors located in Washington, DC, that supervises the system, twelve regional banks, and a Federal Open Market Committee that is responsible for monetary policy.

The Board of Governors of the Federal Reserve System

The federal agency that supervises the Fed system, the **Board of Governors**, is located in Washington, D.C. It is composed of seven members appointed by the President of the United States and confirmed by the senate for fourteen-year terms. The Chair of the Federal Reserve System is chosen from the members of the Board.

The Board of Governors has several functions and is directly involved in designing and directing the US monetary policy. All seven members of the Board are voting members of the Federal Open Market Committee, the committee that sets the monetary policy target. The Board is also responsible for setting the reserve requirements and for controlling the discount rate, the interest rate the Fed charges member banks as lender of last resort. The Board has other responsibilities unrelated to monetary policy. For example, it designs bank supervision policies and publishes information and data on the economy and the financial sector.

The Federal Reserve Banks

Each Federal Reserve Bank serves a district and provides services to local banks and the Treasury. Federal Reserve Banks have nine directors, six chosen by member banks and three chosen by the Board of Governors. Six of the nine directors appoint the bank president. The local Reserve Banks have several functions: they extend discount loans to banks in the district, supervise and examine bank holdings and state-chartered member banks, verify that local banks offer fair and equitable services, clear checks, and destroy and substitute damaged currency. The largest district Fed banks in terms of assets held are the New York Fed, the Chicago Fed, and the San Francisco Fed.

....

TIP: The New York Fed is the only Reserve Bank with a trading floor and it performs the open market operations necessary to implement monetary policy.

....

The Federal Open Market Committee (FOMC)

The FOMC is the committee that decides the monetary policy target (currently the Federal Funds Rate) and is responsible for open market operations. It is composed of 12 members: the seven members of the Board of Governors, the president of the New York Fed, and four of the other Reserve Banks presidents on a rotating basis. The FOMC meets about every six weeks. During its regular meetings, the FOMC discusses current economic conditions and makes policy decisions. At the end of each meeting, the committee issues a statement on the economic outlook and choices of monetary policy.

Current Monetary Management

Central banks can take actions that influence interest rates and the money supply. These actions are called the tools of monetary management and policy. As mentioned earlier, interest rates and the money supply influence many facets of the national economy, such as inflation, output, and employment.

Central banks have no direct control over interest rates and the money supply; however, they have a set of tools they use to control one or more policy instruments that in time can influence interest rates and the money supply.

Tools ➜ Policy Instruments ➜ Money Supply & Interest Rates

The Federal Reserve's current policy instrument of choice is an interbank rate called the **federal funds rate**. The federal funds rate is the interest rate depository institutions (and few other financial intermediaries) charge each other on uncollateralized overnight loans of reserves deposited at the Fed. Between 1979 and 1993, when inflation was the main concern of monetary policy, the Federal Reserve used a monetary aggregate called the **monetary base** as its key policy instrument.

Conventional Tools of Monetary Management and Policy

Historically, the Federal Reserve had three tools it could use to influence interest rates and the money supply: open market operations, the discount rate, and the reserve requirement ratio. In response to the financial crisis of 2008/2009, the bank introduced a fourth conventional tool, the interest on reserves, and temporarily started unconventional actions. The four conventional tools of monetary management and policy are:

- **Open market operations:** Open market operations (OMOs) are purchases or sales of securities on the open market. The Federal Reserve uses dynamic OMOs to change the intermediate target level and defensive OMOs to off-set market driven changes in the intermediate target. Permanent (dynamic) OMOs are outright purchases or sales of securities. To perform temporary (defensive) OMOs, the Federal Reserve uses repurchase agreements (repos) or inverse-repurchase agreements (reverse repos). A repo stipulates that the Fed buys a set of securities from a financial intermediary with the agreement that the seller will buy them back at a set time in the future. In a reverse repo, the roles of the Fed and the financial intermediaries are reversed. The Federal Reserve trades securities with a selected group of large financial intermediaries called the primary dealers.
- **Discount window policies:** The Federal Reserve lends funds to financial intermediaries through its discount window. Healthy banks can borrow any amount of funds at the discount rate (primary credit). Distressed member banks can also borrow funds from the Fed as a lender of last resort (secondary credit), paying a premium of 50 basis points over the discount rate.
- **Reserve requirements:** In the US, all depository institutions must hold reserves for a portion of the funds in their demand deposits. The reserve requirements are designed so that smaller banks have a lower reserve ratio than larger banks. Deposits are divided into a lower tranche (currently up to $110.2 million) with a reserve ratio of 3 percent and a higher tranche with a reserve ratio of 10 percent. The first $11.5 million of deposits are exempt. The tranches amounts are updated yearly to respond to the natural expansion of deposits as the economy grows.
- **Interest on Excess Reserves:** Starting in 2008, the Federal Reserve pays interest on banks' required and excess reserves. The interest on excess reserves (IOER) is an incentive for banks to hold reserves and as such can be used as a monetary policy tool.

Current Management: Managing the Federal Funds Rate

To manage credit conditions and money supply, the Federal Reserve uses the federal funds rate. A higher federal funds rate tightens credit conditions and lowers money supply; a lower federal funds rate eases credit conditions and raises the money supply. The federal funds rate is a market interest rate, and it is driven by changes in banks' demand for reserves and the Federal Reserve's supply of reserves.

The Demand for Reserves

The demand for reserves illustrates the amount of reserves banks wish to hold at different federal funds rates. The demand for reserves is downward sloping in the federal funds rate down to the interest on reserves, where it flattens out. When the federal funds rate is higher than the interest on reserves, a higher federal funds rate raises the opportunity cost of holding reserves and lowers the amount of reserves banks wish to hold. If the federal funds rate drops just below the interest rate on reserves, banks have an arbitrage opportunity as they can borrow funds at the lower federal funds rate and deposit them at the Federal Reserve, which pays the higher interest rate on reserves. So, once the federal funds rate declines all the way down to the interest rate on reserves, banks are happy to hold trillions of dollars in reserves.

Supply of Reserves

The supply of reserves illustrates the amount of reserves the Fed supplies at different levels of the federal funds rates. The Federal Reserve has full control of the supply of reserves when the federal funds rate is below the discount rate. In this scenario, banks find it cheaper to borrow in the federal funds market than directly from the Federal Reserve, and the Fed can use open market operations to control the supply of reserves. However, if the federal funds rate rises above the discount rate, banks find it cheaper to borrow from the discount window, and the Federal Reserve cannot push the federal funds rate any higher.

How the Federal Reserve Controls the Federal Funds Rate

The Federal Reserve has great control over the federal funds rate. However, the tools the Federal Reserve can use to control it depend on the federal funds' current level and the current amount of bank reserves.

If the federal funds rate is above the interest on reserves and below the discount rate: If reserves are scarce, the federal funds rate hovers between the interest on reserves and the discount rate. When the federal funds rate is between the interest on reserve and the discount rate, the Federal Reserve uses open market operations to keep the rate to its desired target level or to move it up or down:

- An **open market purchase** of securities lowers the federal funds rate. A purchase of securities increases the supply of reserves, shifts the supply of reserves curve to the right, and lowers the federal funds rate.
- An **open market sale** of securities decreases the supply of reserves, shifts the supply curve to the left and raises the federal funds rate.

As an alternative, the Federal Reserve could use changes in the reserve requirement ratio to move the federal funds rate. This tool, however, influences banks' demand for reserves and is less precise. A higher reserve ratio increases the demand for reserves, shifts the demand for reserves to the right, and raises the federal funds rate. A lower reserve ratio lowers the demand for reserves, shifts the demand for reserves to the left, and lowers the federal funds rate.

If the federal funds rate is at the discount rate: When the federal funds rate is very close to the discount rate, it loses its sensitivity to open market operations. However, the Fed can still control the federal funds rate by raising or lowering the discount rate. A higher discount rate raises the horizontal portion of the supply of reserves and raises the federal funds rate. A lower discount rate lowers the horizontal portion of the supply of reserves and lowers the federal funds rate.

If the federal funds rate is at the interest on reserves: In response to the financial crisis of 2008/09, the Federal Reserve expanded its balance sheet and the supply of reserves. When the supply of reserves is very abundant, the federal funds rate falls just below the interest on reserves. When the federal funds rate is close to the interest on reserves or lower, it also loses sensitivity to open market operations (unless these are massive). This is the current scenario where banks are holding an unusually large amount of excess reserves. However, the Federal Reserve can still control the federal funds rate by raising or lowering the interest on reserves. A higher interest on reserves raises the demand for reserves, shifts the horizontal portion of the demand for reserves up, and raises the federal funds rate. A lower interest on reserves lowers the demand for reserves, shifts the horizontal portion of the demand for reserves down, and lowers the federal funds rate.

Money Creation

New money is created when a bank uses excess reserves to extend a new loan. Through a multiplicative effect, a $1 loan creates more than $1 in extra money. This multiplicative effect is called the **money multiplier**. The size of the money multiplier depends positively on the reserve ratio and negatively on the excess reserve ratio (excess reserves/deposits) and the currency ratio (desired currency holdings/deposits). Hence, the more excess reserves banks wish to hold and the more currency the public wishes to hold, the smaller the money multiplier and the amount of new money created when an extra $1 of reserves is loaned out.

The Fed, the Monetary Base, and Money Creation

The central bank can influence money supply by injecting or draining reserves from the banking system and by influencing the size of the money multiplier. Between 1979 and 1993, the Federal Reserve tried to tightly control the money supply through changes in the monetary base. The monetary base (also called high-powered money) is the sum of the Fed's liabilities and the US Treasury monetary liabilities. Because Treasury liabilities are a small share of the monetary base and are not actively managed, changes in the Fed's liabilities move the monetary base dollar per dollar.

The Fed's liabilities come in two forms: currency in circulation and banks' reserves. Remember: Currency in circulation is cash in the hands of the public. Also, it is important to remember that some banks hold reserves to meet the Fed's reserve requirements (required reserves) but also to meet depositors' withdrawals and to maintain a sound level of liquidity (excess reserves).

On the asset's side of the Fed's balance sheet, securities (generally bonds issued by the US Treasury, but, after the 2008 financial crises, also other securities) and loans to financial institutions play an important role in money creation.

To raise or lower the monetary base, the Fed uses open market operations. An open market purchase raises the monetary base dollar per dollar, while an open market sale lowers the monetary base dollar per dollar. When the Fed buys (or sells) securities to banks, it also raises (or lowers) banks' reserves dollar per dollar. If the Fed buys or sells securities to a nonbank, the effect of the open market operation on reserves is uncertain as it depends on whether the counterpart deposits (or withdraws) the funds at (from) a bank. Discount loans also raise the borrowed portion of the monetary base. The Fed can use the discount rate to influence the volume of these loans; however, it can't perfectly control this component of the monetary base.

The Fed can also control money supply by influencing the money multiplier. The Fed can influence the money multiplier because, on the one hand, it sets the reserve ratio and, on the other hand, it sets the discount rate and the interest on reserves that in turn influence the excess reserve ratio. A higher reserve ratio lowers the money multiplier. A higher discount rate and/ or IOER rate raise the amount of excess reserves banks wish to hold and lower the money multiplier. However, the Fed cannot perfectly control the money multiplier, as economic conditions also affect the excess reserve ratio and the currency ratio—for example, in the early 1930s, the repeated banking crises pushed people to hold more currency and banks to hold larger excess reserves reducing the size of the money multiplier so severely that the money supply dropped even though the Federal Reserve had expanded the monetary base.

The instability of the money multiplier in periods of banking crisis and in times of swift financial innovation is one of the reasons why the Fed decreased its focus on monetary aggregates when implementing monetary policy.

> **TIP:** The **float,** which is money in the banking system briefly counted twice due to the delay in the Fed's check-clearing process, also affects the monetary base in ways out of the Fed's control.

MONETARY POLICY IN THE UNITED STATES

Monetary policies are actions taken by the monetary authority to reach specific macroeconomic goals, like price stability and stability of financial markets.

Policy Effectiveness

The key idea behind monetary policy is that monetary authorities can influence interest rates and credit availability that, in turn, influence **consumption** and **investment expenditures**, the two largest components of total spending. Since prices and wages are sticky and adjust rather slowly, higher total spending results in higher economic activity and slightly higher inflation, while lower total spending results in slower economic activity and lower inflation.

Monetary policy is very effective when the central bank has good control over interest rates and credit conditions and when private investment and consumption are very sensitive to changes in interest rates or the ease with which families and businesses find financing for their purchases and investment projects.

Because central banks cannot influence total spending directly, it takes time for monetary policy to affect output, employment, and inflation. The time it takes for a change in policy to influence the economy is called the **effectiveness lag**.

Conducting Monetary Policy

In the United States, as stated in the 1977 amendment to the Federal Reserve Act, the goals of monetary policy are **price stability**, **maximum sustainable employment**, and moderate long-term interest rates. These two goals are often referred to as the "dual mandate."

The Federal Reserve pursues its dual mandate of price stability and maximum sustainable employment using two sets of tools called conventional and unconventional tools of monetary policy.

The **conventional tools** of monetary policy are:

- Open market operations
- Reserve requirements
- Discount window policy
- Interest on reserves

The **unconventional tools** of monetary policy were developed by the Federal Reserve in response to the challenges posed by the financial crisis of 2008/2009. The unconventional tools of monetary policy are:

- The expansion of the Federal Reserve balance sheet. This tool is often referred to as Quantitative Easing. Once changes in regular tools had lowered short-term interest rates down to zero, the Federal Reserve started using very large purchases of specific types of securities to directly lower long-term interest rates by altering the overall market demand/ supply. The goal of this tool is to stimulate lending.
- Changes in the composition of the Federal Reserve's balance sheet. While traditionally the Federal Reserve had always traded short-term Treasury securities, in order to lower long-term interest rates and mortgage rates, the Federal Reserve focused its new purchases on mortgage backed securities and long-term Treasury securities.

- Forward guidance. The Federal Reserve significantly increased the information it would provide to the public about its future intentions hoping to help investors form accurate expectations for the future.

Policy Instruments

In regular times, the Federal Reserve uses its conventional tools to influence its policy instrument, the federal funds rate. An operating target is a variable the Federal Reserve can fully control and that can influence short-term interest rates and money supply.

The choice of the federal funds rate has consequences for the money supply. If the Federal Reserve wishes to maintain the federal funds rate at its target level for a while, it must inject reserves when the federal funds rate tends to increase and drain reserves when the federal funds rate tends to decline losing control over the monetary base. Hence, either the Federal Reserve targets the federal funds rate or it targets reserves and the monetary base.

Transmission Channels

In the United States, it takes about one year for monetary policy to influence the level of economic activity and about two years to influence the inflation rate. Monetary policy affects the economy through several channels.

- **Interest rate channel:** Monetary policy affects the real interest rate and fixed investment and consumption of durable goods.
- **Asset prices channels:** Monetary policy affects the value of the currency and asset prices influencing net exports, investment, and consumption.
- **Credit channels:** Monetary policy affects bank deposits and banks' willingness to lend as well as asset prices and firms' and families' ability to post collateral and borrow influencing investment and consumption.

Targets and Strategy

In the United States, the Federal Reserve performs monetary policy with a clear attention to controlling inflation in the long run, however, not with an officially stated inflation rate target. Inflation targeting—setting and communicating an explicit target for inflation and performing monetary policy so as to reach the inflation target at all times—would not allow the Federal Reserve to pursue its dual mandate of price stability and maximum sustainable employment during periods of cost-pushed inflation.

Because of the long time lags between monetary policy actions and the inflation rate response, the Federal Reserve tries to be forward-looking. This strategy has been very successful at containing inflation and allowed the Federal Reserve some flexibility during recessions. This strategy, however, relies very heavily on the prestige and credibility of the central bankers.

Interest Rates and the Impact on Money Supply

As discussed, if the central bank targets interest rates it must adjust the money supply in response to fluctuations in what economists call the money demand—the amount of cash and liquidity the public wishes to hold at every interest rate.

According to the Keynesian "liquidity preference theory," people wish to hold cash and deposits in the bank because they need cash to pay for transactions. However, every dollar kept in the bank is a dollar not invested in stocks and bonds, securities that pay a much higher interest rate than any bank deposit. In economic parlance, the interest rate paid by bonds is an opportunity cost of holding money. Hence, according to the theory, at every interest rate people wish to hold more cash when they need to cover more transactions and at every level of transactions they wish to hold less cash when interest rates are higher.

When the economy is doing well and people have more transactions to pay for, they wish to hold more cash at every interest rate, and money demand increases. If people cannot borrow the extra cash from commercial banks, they get the cash from selling securities like stocks and bonds. As the supply of stocks and bonds increases, asset prices decline. Because there is a negative relationship between asset prices and interest rates (or yields), as asset prices decline, interest rates increase. Hence, more transactions lead to a higher money demand and higher interest rates and fewer transactions lead to a lower money demand and lower interest rates.

If the central bank wishes to keep interest rates somewhat stable, it must inject reserves and increase money supply when money demand increases and drain reserves and lower money supply when money demand declines.

Monetary vs. Fiscal Policy

Monetary policies are actions central banks (or other monetary authorities) take to reach some macroeconomic goals. In the United States, the Federal Reserve has a dual goal of price stability and maximum sustainable employment.

Fiscal policies are discretionary actions a central government—in the United States, the Federal Government—takes to reach certain macroeconomic goals and influence the macroeconomic outlook.

There are three tools of discretionary fiscal policy:

1. *Government purchases:* The federal government can directly influence total spending by increasing or cutting its consumption and investment expenditures or the grants it pays to states.
2. *Public transfers:* public transfers are direct payments to families and businesses like social security pensions or unemployment insurance benefits. Transfers influence disposable income and consumption expenditures, the largest component of total spending.
3. *Taxes:* during economic downturns, the federal government can introduce temporary tax credits or tax cuts that can boost disposable income and consumption.

Governments can reduce economic fluctuations through the use of automatic stabilizers, properties of the tax system and the organization of public expenditures that automatically raise public expenditures and lower taxes during economic downturns and lower public expenditures and raise taxes during inflationary periods. Progressive taxation and generous welfare programs would act as automatic stabilizers. Compared to most European nations, the United States has weaker automatic stabilizers.

When evaluating the relative merits of employing monetary instead of fiscal policy, economists make three considerations:

1. The first consideration is **public policy and the real interest rate**. While an expansionary monetary policy tends to lower the real interest rate stimulating private investment, an expansionary fiscal policy tends to increase the real interest rate depressing private investment an important phenomenon called the **"crowding out"** effect. Typically, government pays for its expansionary fiscal policies by issuing new debt. As government increases its borrowing the supply of loanable funds declines and the real interest rate increases "crowding out" private investment.
2. The second factor to consider: **is fiscal policy at all effective?** Some economists believe that fiscal policy is quite ineffective at stimulating the economy. They believe that when government purchases increase, even if the increase is paid by issuing new debt, families anticipate that some time in the future they will have to pay higher taxes to lower the national debt and therefore decide to increase their saving and reduce consumption.

3. The third consideration is **time lags**. Fiscal policy and monetary policy suffer from different time lags. Monetary policy is fast to decide and implement, but has long effectiveness lags, while fiscal policy has long implementation lags but once implemented it reaches the economy faster than monetary policy.

The Financial Crisis Of 2008/2009

In 2008/2009, the world financial sector experienced a severe financial crisis that triggered a deep economic downturn that economists and commentators have labeled the **Great Recession**. A housing market boom and bust, financial innovation, and problems of moral hazard at loan originators and at credit rating companies all contributed to the crisis.

In the 2000s, financial innovation had channeled trillions of dollars into the market for mortgage loans, increasing the demand for new and existing homes and inflating home prices. Financial intermediaries had found a way to bundle individual mortgage loans into a new type of bond called a mortgage-backed security. This process, called **securitization**, was meant to lower risk; but instead, it reduced mortgage originators' incentive to carefully screen mortgage applicants so that mortgage-backed securities ended up being backed by shaky and risky mortgages. Soon, financial intermediaries started using mortgage-backed securities to build other complex collateralized debt obligations (CDOs). As more and more complex securities hit the market, credit-rating agencies that were earning huge fees advising financial firms on the most profitable way to structure these new financial instruments found themselves in a conflict of interest and their ratings lost all accuracy.

Investors and financial intermediaries who saw mortgage-backed securities receive high ratings thought that CDOs carried little risk and invested heavily in these new obligations. When home prices started falling in 2006, many homeowners could not afford their monthly payments any more and started defaulting on their mortgages, bringing down the value of mortgage-backed securities. Financial intermediaries were heavily invested in these types of securities, which they commonly used as collateral to borrow short-term. As the market for mortgage-backed securities collapsed, some investment banks saw their assets vaporize, as they had to engage in fire sales of assets to keep liquid.

In the United States, the first sign of serious stress came in January 2008 when **Countrywide** financial corp, the largest mortgage bank in the country, failed and was sold to Bank of America. Then in March 2008, **Bear**

Stearns, an investment bank and brokerage firm, collapsed and had to be sold to JP Morgan at a tenth of its value. The most dramatic events, however, took place in September 2008 when within a few days 1) the investment bank **Lehman Brothers** failed, 2) two large Government Sponsored Enterprises (GSEs)—**Fannie Mae and Freddie Mac**—that provided credit to the housing market repurchasing mortgage loans, were taken over by the Treasury, and 3) America's largest insurance company, **AIG**, had to be rescued by the Federal Reserve.

The Federal Reserve and the Treasury took exceptional steps in response to the crisis to prevent financial contagion and to support liquidity. Starting in 2007, the Federal Reserve injected liquidity lowering the discount rate and opened several lending facilities where nonbank financial intermediaries could borrow funds or swap securities and where foreign banks could swap domestic currency for dollars. In 2008, the Bush administration passed the **Economic Recovery Act** that authorized the Treasury to spend $700 billion to get troubled mortgage-backed securities off financial intermediaries' balance sheets or to support their capital in other ways through the **Troubled Assets Relief Plan (TARP)**. In 2009, the Obama administration passed the **American Recovery and Reconstruction Act,** a $750 billion stimulus package to be disbursed over three years.

THE INTERNATIONAL MONETARY SYSTEM

International Banking

Although the Federal Reserve Act of 1913 allowed American banks to open branches abroad and in 1919 the passage of the Edge Act allowed the creation of special corporations that could own portions of foreign financial institutions, American banks started expanding their global activities only in the 1960s.

Banks' interest in foreign operations followed 1) an intensification of US firms' trade with the rest of the world, 2) the expansion of US companies abroad and the rising number of multinational corporations, 3) a desire to escape the stricter regulatory environment typical of the US banking system—in particular, the restrictions on capital outflows imposed in the mid-60s, the old Regulation Q that limited the interest banks could charge on demand deposits, and the limits the Glass-Steagall Act imposed on commercial banks' activities.

US banks can opt for a variety of organizational forms to expand their foreign reach, from representative offices that offer minimal information and assistance services to foreign branches, integral parts of the parent bank, that offer a full range of services. To assist with interbank transactions, an American bank might open a shell branch. These branches do not offer services to the public and are generally located in countries with simple banking regulation, no taxes, a stable political regime, and no currency controls.

Nowadays, foreign bank operations are subject to the larger share of domestic banking regulations. For example, unless they are set up as international banking facilities (IFBs), they must keep required reserves, they can only offer services allowed to domestic banks, and, starting in 2010 with the passage of the Dodd-Frank Act, they can engage in limited trading or speculative activities.

Just like their domestic parents, international branches earn most of their income from extending loans. These are often funded and priced differently from domestic loans. Very large loans are often extended by groups of banks called banks syndicates. Foreign loans expose banks to additional risks. Like all other loans, they expose the bank to interest risk and credit risk; however, unlike domestic loans, they also expose the bank to **currency risk** and **country risk**. If the loan is extended in a foreign currency, the value of the loan is sensitive to changes in the value of the currency. The country risk stems from possible political turmoil in the foreign country where a change in the governing elite could lead to restrictions on foreign loans repayment.

As US banks have expanded their operations abroad, foreign banks have entered the United States banking system. Currently, about 100 foreign banks have offices in the United States; however, the larger ones dominate the market.

TIP: Foreign banks in the United States are subject to very strict oversight from the Federal Reserve and are more limited than US banks in their geographical reach and range of activities.

International Monetary Institutions and Debt Crisis

In July 1944, representatives of the allied forces met at a resort in Bretton Woods, New Hampshire, to design the post-war international system of payments. The delegates agreed that all countries would keep their currencies in a fixed exchange rate regime backed by gold: the **Bretton Woods system**.

To guarantee stability to the new system, the international community agreed to create an organization called the **International Monetary Fund (IMF)**. Under a fixed exchange regime, countries with a balance of payment deficit (in other words, countries that buy abroad more than they sell abroad) lose foreign reserves. As they work to correct the trade and investment imbalances, they need injections of foreign reserves to prop up the value of their currency and maintain the fixed exchange rate. The key role of the IMF was loaning foreign currency to member countries with this type of problem. In the 1970s, increasing inflation in the United States put an end to the fixed exchange rate system and significantly reduced the relevance of the IMF.

However, starting in the mid-1980s, the Fund found a new role as a lender of last resort to countries facing an external debt crisis. In the 1980s, the IMF gave assistance to Latin American countries that in the 1960s and 1970s had accumulated large and unsustainable external debt to pay for development investments. Again, in the mid and late 90s, the IMF provided loans to Mexico and a number of Asian countries that found themselves in a similar position.

Most recently, the Fund helped more than fifty countries respond to the financial crisis of 2008/2009, including a number of European countries whose governments were unable to repay their debt to foreign investors and foreign banks. The IMF raises funds through a quota system. Each member country deposits a quota proportional to the nation's contribution to global GDP that is paid in a mix of hard currencies (US dollar, Euro, Yen, etc.), domestic currency, and **Special Drawing Rights**, a fiat currency used solely to extend IMF loans. After the financial crisis of 2008/2009, the IMF significantly modified and expanded the types of loans offered to member countries.

Other Important International Monetary System Institutions

- **The World Bank:** The World Bank is one of the organizations created at the Bretton Woods conference in 1944. The original goal of the bank was financing the European reconstruction efforts at the end of WWII. Today, the bank is a group of organizations that offers loans and other assistance for development projects in low-income and middle-income countries with the overarching goal of ending extreme poverty in the world.

- **The Bank for International Settlements (BIS):** Created in 1930 and based in Basel, Switzerland, the Bank for International Settlements fosters cooperation among monetary authorities with the overarching goal of pursuing the stability of domestic and global financial markets.
- **The World Trade Organization:** The World Trade Organization is an organization of governments that negotiates and renegotiates international trade agreements. It was created in 1995 and substitutes the General Agreement on Tariffs and Trade (GATT) negotiation rounds. The overarching goal is to reduce barriers to international trade.
- **The Euro zone and the ECB:** The Euro zone is a monetary union of nineteen European countries that share a common currency called the Euro. While each country maintains a separate central bank, a central authority called the European Central Bank (ECB) decides and implements the zone's monetary policy.

International Payments and Exchange Rates

Foreign exchange markets are trades of deposits denominated in different currencies. The price of one currency in terms of another is called the **foreign exchange rate**. Trades between individuals or firms and domestic banks are called the retail foreign exchange market while interbank trades of very large deposits are called the interbank or wholesale foreign exchange market. Unlike stocks that are traded in exchanges (for example, the New York Stock Exchange), currencies are traded directly over-the-counter among hundreds of dealers and each transaction is generally for more than $1 million.

Currencies can be traded in spot markets where bank deposits are exchanged immediately or in forward markets where deposits are exchanged at a chosen date in the future.

When the price of the domestic currency in terms of a foreign currency increases, economists use the term domestic currency appreciation. When the price of the domestic currency in terms of a foreign currency declines, the domestic currency is depreciating.

The foreign exchange rate is very important to an economy as it influences net exports and sales and purchases of securities. When the domestic currency appreciates, domestic goods become relatively more expensive than foreign goods and exports of domestic goods decline while imports of foreign goods rise.

> **TIP:** In a formula, suppose P is the domestic price level, P* is the foreign price level, and E is the price of domestic currency in foreign currency. Then, according to the purchasing power parity theory: $P = E \times P^*$.

Forces That Drive the Foreign Exchange Rate

The foreign exchange rate is a price, and, like all prices, it fluctuates in response to changes in demand and supply. Other things staying the same, when the demand for domestic currency increases, the domestic currency appreciates and the price of the domestic currency in terms of the foreign currency rises. For example, a higher demand for dollars paid in Euros appreciates the dollar; it depreciates the Euro and raises the number of Euros one must pay to buy one dollar. When the supply of the domestic currency increases, the domestic currency depreciates and the price of the domestic currency in terms of the foreign currency declines.

The forces behind long-term movements in the foreign exchange rate are different from those that shape day-to-day fluctuations. In the long run, the foreign exchange rate is driven by changes in international trade. Economists track the long run behavior of the foreign exchange rate using the **purchasing power parity theory**. According to this theory, people must be indifferent to buying the same item domestically or internationally, as changes in imports and exports triggered by a misalignment of domestic and foreign prices would move the exchange rate in a equilibrating direction.

According to the purchasing power theory, in the long run, the foreign exchange rate is driven by:

- **The domestic price level:** If the domestic price level increases, domestic goods become less competitive compared to foreign goods and the demand for dollars declines, leading to a depreciation of the dollar.
- **The foreign price level:** If the foreign price level increases, domestic goods become more competitive compared to foreign goods and the demand for dollars rises, leading to an appreciation of the dollar.
- **Relative productivity:** If productivity in the United States grows faster than abroad, US items become cheaper than foreign items and the demand for dollars increases, so that the dollar appreciates.
- **Tariffs and other trade barriers:** The introduction or increase of tariffs and other trade barriers raise the demand for domestic goods compared to foreign goods, so that the domestic currency appreciates.

In the short run, the demand and the supply of domestic currency is driven by the relative return of investing in domestic assets compared to investing in foreign assets. Financial investors compare the domestic interest rate to the foreign interest rate controlling for the effect of a possible appreciation of the domestic currency.

- **The domestic interest rate:** A higher domestic interest rate increases the relative demand for domestic assets and the demand for the domestic currency leading to an appreciation of the domestic currency.
- **The foreign interest rate:** A higher foreign interest rate decreases the relative demand for domestic assets and the demand for the domestic currency leading to a depreciation of the domestic currency.
- **Changes in the expected appreciation of the domestic currency:** An appreciation of the domestic currency lowers the rate of return in domestic currency paid by securities denominated in foreign currency. If investors now expect a faster appreciation of the domestic currency, they demand relatively more domestic assets, raising the demand for the domestic currency and leading the domestic currency to appreciate.

The Balance of Payments (BoP)

The balance of payments is an accounting tool that tallies a country's transactions with the rest of the world. Transactions that create an inflow of payments (e.g., exports of domestic goods) are called **credits**, while transactions that create an outflow of payments (e.g., imports of foreign goods) are called **debits**.

Transactions are divided into three accounts:

- **The current account** tallies flows of payments from 1) the purchase or sale of goods and services, 2) earnings on financial investment and from labor earnings, and 3) unilateral payments like remittances and direct foreign aid. The value of exports minus the value of imports is called the trade balance.
- **The financial account** tallies payments from the purchase and sale of investment assets like securities or real estate. Flows of government-owned reserves, including special drawing rights (SDRs), are also tallied here. The financial account measures a country's net borrowing from abroad as the difference between the net sale of domestic assets abroad. A positive net sale indicates an inflow of payments and an increase in net borrowing, and so it's a BoP credit—and the net repayment of liabilities abroad. A positive net repayment of liabilities indicates an outflow of payments and a decline in net borrowing, and so it's a BoP debit.

- The capital account tallies payments from the purchase or sale of nonfinancial assets or nonproduced items, for example land or intellectual property rights.

Aside from statistical discrepancies (that at times can be significant), the balance of payment is equal to zero, as the name suggests. The capital account is very small, and deficits of the current account are compensated by surpluses of the financial account. If a country runs a current account deficit, perhaps because it imports more than it exports, it can pay for the difference by selling domestic assets and increasing net borrowing, by drawing down on foreign reserves, or by selling domestic currency for foreign currency. All of these actions lead to a surplus in the financial account that keeps the BoP balanced.

Monetary Policy in Conjunction With the Exchange Rate

The effectiveness of monetary policy depends on a country's foreign exchange regime.

The Fixed Exchange Rate Policy Trilemma

A country that wants to maintain a fixed parity against one or more other currencies faces a fixed exchange rates policy trilemma: the three policies of fixed exchange rates, open capital markets, and control over monetary policy cannot coexist.

Monetary policy is effective only when it can influence the real interest rate. However, if a country has open financial capital markets, movements of the real interest rate change the inflow and outflow of financial securities shifting the demand and the supply of the domestic currency. So either the central bank allows the foreign exchange rate to fluctuate in response to these movements in demand and supply, or it buys domestic currency when there is a surplus and sells domestic currency when there is a shortage, actions that influence the size and direction of monetary policy. With open financial capital markets, the central bank must choose between fixed exchange rates and control over its monetary policy.

Monetary Policy with a Foreign Exchange Rate Float

A country that allows its currency to fluctuate against other currencies enjoys a particularly effective monetary policy.

In a closed economy, that is an economy that does not trade goods or securities with the rest of the world, monetary policy influences the economy only through changes in investment and consumption.

In an open economy with a fluctuating foreign exchange rate, monetary policy influences the economy also through changes in net exports triggered by movements in the foreign exchange. For example, if the central bank wants to raise output and employment and lowers the real interest rate, in an open economy, the resulting outflow of financial capital depreciates the domestic currency stimulating net exports, adding an extra channel to the transmission mechanism.

SUMMING IT UP

- Money is an **asset**, or a durable item with value that is accepted as a means of payment.
- Assets that can be used as money include **durable assets** (which last over time), **acceptable assets** (which are convenient for people to use), **divisible assets** (which can be divided into smaller units), and **fungible assets** (which are similar to every other unit so that they can be used interchangeably).
- The four key roles of money are as a **means of payment**, as a **store of value**, as a **standard of deferred payment**, and as a **unit of accounting**.
- The three types of money are **commodity money** (like gold and silver), **commodity backed money** (money aligned to the gold standard), and **fiat money** (paper certificates not backed by gold or any other commodity), which makes up most money today.
- **Financial assets** include **money** (assets that derive value from a contract), **loans** (financial assets that derive value from a repayment contract), and **securities** (financial assets that can be traded).
    - ⊛ **Securities are traded in primary markets, secondary markets**, and open markets, and have three classes:
        1. Debt securities (bank notes and bonds)
        2. Equity securities (common stocks)
        3. Derivatives (event-based money flow which includes futures, options, and stocks)

- Financial assets often pay **interest**, or additional payments made on top of the principal amount loaned at the start $(I = (N - M))$. The interest rate is the ratio of interest to principal, or $I = \dfrac{N - M}{M}$. Interest can be difficult to calculate in the case of fixed payment loans, like mortgage loans or coupon bonds, so the yield to maturity method is used. This is the interest rate that equates the current price of a debt security or loan to the present discounted value of all payments the lender will receive from the security or loan at maturity.

- The **US banking sector** is characterized by three things: a **large number of small banks, banks chartered at two levels** (state and national), and **heavy regulation**. These regulations included the Glass-Steagall Act of 1933 (which limited banks' activities and interest rate charges) and the Gramm-Leach-Bliley Act of 1999 (which replaced Glass-Steagall and enabled banks to participate in nonbank financial activities).

- The three main types of banks in the United States are **commercial banks**, **Saving Associations/Savings and Loans Associations**, and **credit unions**. Deposits at these banks are insured for up to $250,000 per account by the Federal Deposit Insurance Corporation (FDIC) or the National Credit Union Share Insurance Fund (NCUSIF). In addition to banks, the most important types of financial companies are investment banks (which raise funds via securities); insurance companies (which help protect people from potential losses in exchange for a fixed premium payment); mutual funds/pension funds (which are pools of funds invested in securities); and bank holding companies (which own other banks).

- **Banks' assets are their liabilities plus their capital.** Liabilities include: demand deposits, savings deposits, time deposits, borrowed funds, federal funds, repurchase agreements (repos), Eurodollars, Federal Reserve (Fed) loans, and trading liabilities. A bank's capital (a.k.a. "net worth") includes capital stock invested by stockholders and undivided profits that haven't yet been paid out as dividends. Assets are measured by cash assets, Fed funds/reverse repos, investments, loans, and leases.

- **Bank management** is made up of **liquidity management** (where a bank must have enough reserves to meet a minimum requirement and be able to pay out any customer withdrawals), **asset management** (where the bank monitors its asset portfolio to minimize the risk of default), **liability management** (attracting new funds at low cost/low risk), **capital adequacy management** (ensuring the bank has enough capital), and **risk management** (adjusting assets, liabilities, and capital to be able to minimize losses and risk without endangering profits).

- Banks are regulated in four main areas. **Capital requirements** (minimum amounts of capital on hand) are a buffer that help ensure banks won't fail. **Charters** (licenses) are legally required to ensure that banks meet industry requirements, and banks are inspected and rated on an ongoing basis to make sure they're in compliance with that charter. **Disclosure requirements** ensure transparency about the health and activities of a bank. **Regulations** like the Consumer Credit Protection Act and the Fair Credit Billing Act (FCBA) are designed to protect consumers from scams, discrimination, and predatory lending practices.

- The value of all final goods and services produced for the market over a period of time is the **Gross Domestic Product** (GDP), which is made up of **consumption** (money spent on goods), **investment** (money spent on residential and nonresidential structures), **government spending**, and **net exports** (the difference between exports to other nations and imports from other nations). Income is tracked via **Net National Income (NNI)** (wages and salaries, rents, interest and profit), and is further refined into **disposable income (DI)**, which is the difference between NNI and taxes.

- Price levels, or the average of all prices, are tracked using the **Consumer Price Index (CPI)** or the **Personal Consumption Expenditures deflator (PCE deflator)**. Inflation is continual and generalized increase in the price level, and inflation rate measures how fast the prices are increasing.

- Remember the three theories of economics:
  1. In **classical economics**, the economy is seen as self-regulating and calls for a laissez-faire approach, because supply creates its own demand and eliminates the need for government involvement.
  2. In **Keynesian economics**, the economy can't self-adjust and calls for government spending and public policy to maintain economic equilibrium.
  3. In **monetarist economics**, fiscal policy affects the economy in the short term, while affecting prices and inflation in the long term.

- **Inflation can be broken down into three theories.** In the **quantity theory of inflation**, high money growth leads to faster inflation. In **demand-pull inflation**, higher money supply lowers interest rates, thus stimulating investment and consumption (total spending). In **cost push inflation**, increased production costs lead to inflation.

- The central bank in the United States is the **Federal Reserve**, which was created in 1913 to bring stability to the country's banking system, streamline check collection, and supervise the banking industry. The bank has the power to issue Federal Reserve notes, which can be converted to gold and used to maintain elastic currency. The Federal Reserve System is made up of twelve regional banks, a Board of Governors, and a Federal Open Market Committee and is overseen by a Chair appointed by the President and approved by Congress. Federal Reserve notes that could be converted into gold and used to maintain elastic currency.

- The **Federal Reserve** uses three tools to influence interest rates and money supply:
  1. *Open market operations* (sales or purchases of securities on the open market)
  2. *Discount window policies* (funds lent by the Federal Reserve to banks at a discount)
  3. *The reserve requirement ratio* (the percentage of deposits that banks must keep on hand in order to cover withdrawals)
- The Fed also uses the **federal funds rate** (a market interest rate driven by the supply and demand for reserves) to manage credit and money supply. If this rate is above the interest on reserves and below the discount rate, it is lowered by open market purchases of securities and raised by open market sales of securities. If the rate is at the discount rate or is at the interest on reserves, it is not affected by open market operations.
- **Money supply** is the sum of currency in circulation and checkable deposits (M1). New money is created when a bank uses excess reserves to extend a new loan, resulting in the money multiplier effect, where a $1 loan creates more than $1 in new money. Money supply is also affected by the Fed's actions to inject or drain reserves from the banking system and influence the size of the money multiplier.
- Per the 1977 amendment to the Federal Reserve Act, the **goals of monetary policy** are **price stability, maximum sustainable employment**, and **moderate long-term interest rates**.
- The **conventional tools of monetary policy** are **open market operations, reserve requirements, discount window policy**, and **interest on reserves**.
- **Unconventional tools of monetary policy** (developed in response to the 2008/2009 financial crisis) are **expansion of the Federal Reserve's balance sheet, changing the composition of the Federal Reserve's balance sheet**, and **forward guidance/information** from the Federal Reserve to the public.
- **Fiscal policy** (government spending and taxation) consists of government purchases, public transfers (payments like Social Security or unemployment benefits), and taxes (including tax credits or cuts).
- The **Great Recession of 2008–2009** came on the heels of a severe financial crisis caused by a housing boom and bust, financial innovation leading to risky mortgage loans, and the collapse of major mortgage, investment, and credit companies.

- Emergency measures included relief and stimulus bills to help stabilize at-risk banks and companies:
  - The Economic Recovery Act
  - Troubled Assets Relief Plan (TARP)
  - The American Recovery and Reconstruction Act
- American banks began expanding global banking activities in the 1960s, following increased global trade, the expansion of US companies abroad, and companies' desire to escape the US's strict regulations. As a result of the expansion, foreign banks began entering the US as well.
- After World War II, the **International Monetary Fund** (**IMF**) was established to ensure that all countries kept their currencies in a fixed exchange rate regime backed by gold. The IMF ensures economic stability throughout the world by raising funds through a quota system.
- Other international monetary institutions include the **World Bank** (which offers loans and assistance for projects in developing countries), the **Bank for International Settlements** (**BIS**) (which fosters cooperation between monetary authorities to maintain market stability), the **World Trade Organization** (**WTO**) (which negotiates international trade agreements), and the **Euro Zone/ECB** (which provides a common currency for nineteen European nations).
- The **foreign exchange rate** (price of one currency in terms of another currency) is an essential piece of a national economy, as it influences net exports and the sale/purchase of securities. The rate is driven by changes in international trade (domestic price level, foreign price level, relative productivity, and tariffs/trade considerations) in the long run. In the short run, the rate is driven by the relative return of investing in domestic assets compared to investing in foreign assets (domestic interest rate, foreign interest rate, and shifts in domestic currency).

Chapter 4

Money and Banking Post-Test

POST-TEST ANSWER SHEET

1. Ⓐ Ⓑ Ⓒ Ⓓ	18. Ⓐ Ⓑ Ⓒ Ⓓ	35. Ⓐ Ⓑ Ⓒ Ⓓ
2. Ⓐ Ⓑ Ⓒ Ⓓ	19. Ⓐ Ⓑ Ⓒ Ⓓ	36. Ⓐ Ⓑ Ⓒ Ⓓ
3. Ⓐ Ⓑ Ⓒ Ⓓ	20. Ⓐ Ⓑ Ⓒ Ⓓ	37. Ⓐ Ⓑ Ⓒ Ⓓ
4. Ⓐ Ⓑ Ⓒ Ⓓ	21. Ⓐ Ⓑ Ⓒ Ⓓ	38. Ⓐ Ⓑ Ⓒ Ⓓ
5. Ⓐ Ⓑ Ⓒ Ⓓ	22. Ⓐ Ⓑ Ⓒ Ⓓ	39. Ⓐ Ⓑ Ⓒ Ⓓ
6. Ⓐ Ⓑ Ⓒ Ⓓ	23. Ⓐ Ⓑ Ⓒ Ⓓ	40. Ⓐ Ⓑ Ⓒ Ⓓ
7. Ⓐ Ⓑ Ⓒ Ⓓ	24. Ⓐ Ⓑ Ⓒ Ⓓ	41. Ⓐ Ⓑ Ⓒ Ⓓ
8. Ⓐ Ⓑ Ⓒ Ⓓ	25. Ⓐ Ⓑ Ⓒ Ⓓ	42. Ⓐ Ⓑ Ⓒ Ⓓ
9. Ⓐ Ⓑ Ⓒ Ⓓ	26. Ⓐ Ⓑ Ⓒ Ⓓ	43. Ⓐ Ⓑ Ⓒ Ⓓ
10. Ⓐ Ⓑ Ⓒ Ⓓ	27. Ⓐ Ⓑ Ⓒ Ⓓ	44. Ⓐ Ⓑ Ⓒ Ⓓ
11. Ⓐ Ⓑ Ⓒ Ⓓ	28. Ⓐ Ⓑ Ⓒ Ⓓ	45. Ⓐ Ⓑ Ⓒ Ⓓ
12. Ⓐ Ⓑ Ⓒ Ⓓ	29. Ⓐ Ⓑ Ⓒ Ⓓ	46. Ⓐ Ⓑ Ⓒ Ⓓ
13. Ⓐ Ⓑ Ⓒ Ⓓ	30. Ⓐ Ⓑ Ⓒ Ⓓ	47. Ⓐ Ⓑ Ⓒ Ⓓ
14. Ⓐ Ⓑ Ⓒ Ⓓ	31. Ⓐ Ⓑ Ⓒ Ⓓ	48. Ⓐ Ⓑ Ⓒ Ⓓ
15. Ⓐ Ⓑ Ⓒ Ⓓ	32. Ⓐ Ⓑ Ⓒ Ⓓ	49. Ⓐ Ⓑ Ⓒ Ⓓ
16. Ⓐ Ⓑ Ⓒ Ⓓ	33. Ⓐ Ⓑ Ⓒ Ⓓ	50. Ⓐ Ⓑ Ⓒ Ⓓ
17. Ⓐ Ⓑ Ⓒ Ⓓ	34. Ⓐ Ⓑ Ⓒ Ⓓ	51. Ⓐ Ⓑ Ⓒ Ⓓ

52. Ⓐ Ⓑ Ⓒ Ⓓ   55. Ⓐ Ⓑ Ⓒ Ⓓ   58. Ⓐ Ⓑ Ⓒ Ⓓ

53. Ⓐ Ⓑ Ⓒ Ⓓ   56. Ⓐ Ⓑ Ⓒ Ⓓ   59. Ⓐ Ⓑ Ⓒ Ⓓ

54. Ⓐ Ⓑ Ⓒ Ⓓ   57. Ⓐ Ⓑ Ⓒ Ⓓ   60. Ⓐ Ⓑ Ⓒ Ⓓ

MONEY AND BANKING POST-TEST

72 minutes—60 questions

Directions: Carefully read each of the following 60 questions. Choose the best answer to each question and fill in the corresponding circle on the answer sheet. The Answer Key and Explanations can be found following this post-test.

---

1. In many countries, central authorities impose reserve requirements to influence money supply and help prevent bank runs. In the United States, reserve requirements are decided by the

   A. Board of Governors of the Federal Reserve System.
   B. Federal Open Market Committee (FOMC).
   C. Office of the Comptroller of the Currency (OCC).
   D. Federal Deposit Insurance Corporation (FDIC).

2. In the United States, the central authorities that provide liquidity guarantees and credit guarantees are the

   A. OCC and the state regulatory agencies.
   B. OCC and the FDIC.
   C. Federal Reserve Bank and the OCC.
   D. Federal Reserve Bank and the FDIC.

3. When a central bank implements monetary policy so as to target the interest rate

   A. it also implicitly targets the monetary aggregate M1.
   B. the money supply becomes pro-cyclical.
   C. the money supply becomes anti-cyclical.
   D. banks are more reluctant to lend funds to families and small businesses.

4. Which of the following is an example of "asset transformation"?

A. A bank signs a repurchase agreement with another financial intermediary.

B. A financial intermediary chooses the stocks and bonds to include in a new growth-oriented mutual fund.

C. A commercial bank accepts a new NOW deposit and uses the funds to offer a mortgage to a homeowner.

D. A bank sells $100 million of mortgage-backed securities and uses the proceeds of the sale to buy $100 million of Treasury notes.

5. What does the term "quantitative easing" refer to?

A. When the Federal Reserve buys bonds from the Treasury to ease government's budget problems

B. When the Federal Reserve injects reserves when interest rates are rising and lowers reserves when interest rates are low

C. When the Federal Reserve eases credit by increasing the quantity of funds that intermediaries can borrow through its primary credit facility

D. When the Federal Reserve buys large amounts of securities from financial institutions to increase liquidity in the financial system and stimulate lending

6. Which of the following products offered by commercial banks is NOT covered by FDIC insurance?

A. A money market mutual fund

B. A money market deposit account

C. A certificate of deposit

D. A savings account

7. According to monetarist and Keynesian economists, monetary policy is more effective at stimulating total output

A. when private investment spending is more sensitive to credit conditions and the interest rate.

B. when consumption spending is less sensitive to total output and net taxes.

C. when the central bank has little control over interest rates.

D. in the longer run than in the shorter run.

8. The Board of Governors is the key player in monetary policy decisions because

   A. it's the branch of the Federal Reserve System with banking supervision authority.

   B. it creates and publishes statistics on current economic conditions.

   C. its seven members have voting rights in the Federal Open Market Committee (FOMC).

   D. it chooses the target level for the Federal Funds Rate.

9. On September 25, 2008, when the FDIC transferred all of the failing Washington Mutual's assets and liabilities to JP Morgan Chase, it was following which approach to failing banks' resolutions?

   A. Payoff and dissolve

   B. Liquidate and resolve

   C. Whole bank purchase and assumption

   D. Clean bank purchase and assumption

10. Before 2008, which of the following actions would the Federal Reserve take in order to increase the money supply?

   A. It would increase the interest paid on reserves.

   B. It would purchase Treasury securities on the open market.

   C. It would increase the discount rate.

   D. It would increase the required reserve ratio.

11. In the US Balance of Payment, interest on German Treasury securities paid to an American mutual fund is recorded as a

   A. credit in the financial account.

   B. debit in the capital account.

   C. credit in the current account.

   D. debit in the financial account.

12. Which of the following is an action taken by the US Treasury in response to the financial crisis of 2008/2009?

   A. Capital injections under the Troubled Asset Relief Plan

   B. The institution of a new Term Auction Facility that lent funds to financial intermediaries in trouble

   C. The extension of loans to the American International Group (AIG) to avoid the company's failure

   D. The sale of the investment bank Bear Stearns to J.P. Morgan

13. Why did monetarists like Milton Friedman favor strict rules of monetary policy?

    A. They believed that fiscal policy was a better tool for discretionary actions.

    B. They believed that monetary policy affected the economy with long lags.

    C. They believed that monetary policy had no effect on total spending or total output.

    D. They believed that discretionary monetary policy would lead to deflation.

14. The Federal Reserve System is made up of _____ regional Reserve Banks, the Board of Governors, and the _____.

    A. twelve; FOMC

    B. twelve; FDIC

    C. twenty; FOMC

    D. twenty; FDIC

15. When you agree with your employer that at the end of the week he will pay you $1,000 for your work, you use money as a

    A. store of value.

    B. standard of deferred payment.

    C. unit of account.

    D. means of payment.

16. Which of the following lifted limits on interstate banking?

    A. Regulation Q and the Glass-Steagall Act

    B. The McFadden Act

    C. The Depository Institutions Deregulation and Monetary Control Act

    D. The Riegle-Neal Interstate Banking Act

17. If a central bank lowers the primary credit rate, we should expect the money supply to

A. increase as banks will borrow more funds from the Federal Reserve, raising the borrowed monetary base.

B. increase as banks will buy more securities from the Federal Reserve, raising the unborrowed monetary base.

C. decrease as banks will now hold more excess reserves for precautionary purposes, and the money multiplier will decline.

D. decrease as the public will now want to hold less currency, and the money multiplier will decline.

18. Which of the following is the most liquid asset?

A. A plot of land

B. A deposit in a checkable account

C. Shares in a retail money-market mutual fund

D. A deposit in a savings account

19. How does an increase of the required reserve ratio influence the money supply?

A. After the Federal Reserve increases the required reserve ratio to achieve compliance, banks reduce the amount of demand deposits, and the money supply declines.

B. A higher required reserve ratio increases banks' incentive to hold reserves, and the money supply increases.

C. A higher required reserve ratio raises banks' leverage ratio and the public's trust in the stability of the banking sector, reducing the public's currency holding ratio and increasing the money supply.

D. A higher required reserve ratio reduces the share of reserves that banks can loan out, slowing the money creation process and lowering the money supply.

20. In the CAMELS rating system, the C stands for

A. capital adequacy.

B. credit availability.

C. currency holdings.

D. consumer protection enforcement.

21. The problem with a bank crisis is that as more and more people withdraw cash from their bank deposits,

   A. the volume of currency in circulation rises and the money supply expands.
   B. the volume of required reserves declines and banks, to avoid accumulating too many excess reserves, start offering riskier loans.
   C. the balance sheet of the Federal Reserve shrinks and monetary base declines.
   D. unless the Federal Reserve increases the monetary base, banks start calling in loans and the money supply drops.

22. The idea that people adjust their price and inflation expectations slowly is called

   A. rational expectations.
   B. hyperbolic expectations.
   C. slow-response expectations.
   D. adaptive expectations.

23. In the past century, the number of commercial banks in the United States has

   A. steadily increased, even if the number of bank branches has remained the same.
   B. remained stable at around 6,000 institutions.
   C. declined up to the mid-seventies and increased ever since.
   D. steadily declined, although the number of bank branches has increased.

24. The equation of exchange states that

   A. in the Balance of Payment the current account and the financial account always sum to zero.
   B. when trading with the rest of the world, the price of a domestic item must equal the price in domestic currency of a foreign item.
   C. the stock of money in the economy times the velocity of money is equal to income at current prices.
   D. in an exchange, different units of the same product must be traded at the same price.

25. When Joanna withdraws $1,000 from her money market mutual fund and deposits the money in her checking account,

A. M1 increases and M2 decreases.
B. M1 increases and M2 stays the same.
C. M1 and M2 decrease.
D. M1 and M2 stay the same.

26. A difference between commercial banks and credit unions is that commercial banks are

A. allowed to accept deposits, while credit unions are not.
B. stock-owned, while credit unions are mutual institutions.
C. generally quite small with deposits of less than $100 million, while credit unions are very large financial intermediaries.
D. chartered by states, while credit unions are regulated by the Comptroller of the Currency.

27. Gross domestic product is the sum of which of the following components?

A. Consumption and savings
B. Disposable income and net taxes
C. Consumption, investment, net taxes, and net exports
D. Consumption, investment, government purchases, and net exports

28. The larger share of commercial banks' assets is in the form of

A. equity capital.
B. loans.
C. security investments.
D. deposits.

29. Both classical economists and the Keynesian economists believe that

    A. all markets are competitive and that prices are flexible and fluctuate to maintain demand equal to supply in every market.
    B. fiscal policy is ineffective in reducing the level of unemployment.
    C. monetary policy is ineffective in maintaining price stability.
    D. in the long run, the economy operates at its potential level where all resources are fully employed.

30. Current capital adequacy regulation requires that a bank's

    A. ratio of Tier 1 and Tier 2 capital to risk-weighted assets be at least 8 percent.
    B. leverage ratio be at least 8 percent.
    C. Tier 1 capital be at least 3 percent.
    D. ratio of Tier 1 to Tier 2 capital be at least 3 percent.

31. A higher inflation rate leads to a lower level of total spending because when inflation increases

    A. the purchase power of real wages declines and firms lower output.
    B. the central bank raises the interest rate dampening investment spending and consumption spending.
    C. business confidence declines and firms drop all investment projects.
    D. firms find it harder to finance research and development projects slowing the pace of technological change.

32. What is an unintended consequence of the regulation introduced by the CRA?

    A. Banks cannot pay interest on demand deposits and find it hard to compete with money market mutual funds.
    B. Financially weak families are offered mortgages they cannot repay and end up losing their homes.
    C. Insured depositors do not feel the need to closely monitor banks' manager behavior, and banks end up taking too much risk.
    D. During a financial crisis, the mark-to-market accounting requirements force financial intermediaries to mark down their assets, exposing them to bank runs.

33. If economic agents have rational expectations, then

    A. anticipated monetary policy has no effect on prices and inflation.

    B. the economy cannot suffer from demand pull inflation.

    C. the economy cannot suffer from cost push inflation.

    D. anticipated fiscal policy has no effect on GDP and employment.

34. A reason why a monetary policy might not be fully effective in stabilizing the economy is that

    A. the central bank has no control over short-term interest rates.

    B. monetary policy has a long effectiveness lag.

    C. monetary policy has a long implementation lag.

    D. total spending is not sensitive to the interest rate.

35. Which of the following statements best explains an unintended consequence of the National Bank Acts?

    A. State banks started relying very heavily on demand deposits as their primary source of liquidity.

    B. The number of state banks quickly declined, so that nowadays, all US banks are nationally chartered.

    C. The number of different currencies used for payments declined significantly.

    D. The Federal Reserve Bank lost control over state banks.

36. The Federal Deposit Insurance Corporation was established in _____ by the _____.

    A. 1933; Glass-Steagall Act

    B. 1933; Federal Reserve Act

    C. 1913; Federal Reserve Act

    D. 1980; McFadden Act

37. Which of the following men championed the creation of the First Bank of the United States?

    A. Andrew Jackson

    B. Alexander Hamilton

    C. John Maynard Keynes

    D. Milton Friedman

38. Which of the following would be an example of banks' increasing reliance on off-balance sheet activities?

A. Banks have increased the number and type of loans they extend each year.

B. Since the financial crisis, banks have expanded their holdings of excess reserves deposited at the Fed.

C. Banks are more likely to resell loans right after origination instead of holding them until maturity.

D. Banks are expanding their holdings of mortgage-backed securities.

39. What do economists refer to when they talk about the "policy trilemma"?

A. The impossibility of having floating exchange rates, a democratic political system, and a deficit in the trade balance

B. The impossibility of having a trade balance deficit when running a public budget deficit

C. That in an open economy, the monetary authority can only use one of the three tools of monetary policy

D. That a country cannot have a fixed exchange rate, open capital markets, and control of monetary policy

40. The Board of Governors influences who is appointed President at each regional Reserve Banks by

A. directly appointing the President of each regional Reserve Bank.

B. making a recommendation to the President of the United States, who then appoints the President of each regional Reserve Bank.

C. appointing three members of the regional Reserve Banks' Board of Directors, which then appoints the Bank's President.

D. making recommendations to the Bank's Board of Directors, which then appoints the Bank's President.

41. Which of the following is NOT a tool of monetary policy?

A. Large-scale asset purchases

B. The interbank rate

C. The interest on reserves

D. The discount rate

42. Which of the following statements best describes the concept of real interest rate?

    A. The difference between the market interest rate and the rate of inflation borrowers and lenders believe will prevail over the duration of the loan

    B. The difference between the market interest rate and banks' cost of money

    C. The interest rate that banks charge on loans collateralized by a piece of real estate

    D. The difference between the domestic interest rate and the foreign interest rate after adjusting for the expected appreciation of the currency

43. An open market purchase of treasury securities

    A. increases the monetary base but decreases the money supply.

    B. increases the monetary base and increases the money supply.

    C. decreases the monetary base and decreases the money supply.

    D. decreases the monetary base but increases the money supply.

44. After 2009, if the FOMC announced its intention to raise the federal funds rate target by 25 basis points, the next day, the

    A. trading floor of the New York Federal Reserve Bank would perform a sale of Treasury securities on the open market.

    B. Board of Governors would raise the interest on reserves by 25 basis points.

    C. Board of Governors would lower the required reserve ratio applied to the first tranche of funds from 3 percent to 0 percent.

    D. FOMC would raise the primary discount rate by 25 basis points.

45. Which of the following is NOT an example of a fiscal policy?

    A. During recessions, unemployment benefits expenditure increases, driven by higher unemployment.

    B. The administration temporarily cuts income taxes.

    C. The federal government temporarily increases grants to states.

    D. The Federal Reserve purchases Treasury securities.

46. What is the main point of the purchase power parity theory of the foreign exchange rate?

    A. In reality, the law of one price rarely holds.

    B. When the depreciation of the currency raises, prices and wages also increase, so that workers' purchase power remains unaffected.

    C. The foreign exchange rate moves to maintain the parity between the domestic interest rate, the foreign interest rate, and the expected appreciation of the currency.

    D. The foreign exchange moves so as to maintain the parity between an item's domestic price and its foreign price in domestic currency.

47. Which of the following statements best describes how the FDIC contributes to the stability of the financial sector?

    A. The FDIC has the authority to act as lender of last resort to member banks and inject liquidity when money markets dry up.

    B. The FDIC reduces the chances that a bank's failure could trigger a bank run by insuring bank deposits.

    C. The FDIC reduces uncertainty in financial markets by resolving all bank failures following a payoff and liquidate approach.

    D. The FDIC regulates commercial banks' capital requirements so as to minimize systemic risk.

48. Which of the following statements best explains the "crowding out" effect?

    A. Higher public spending creates fears of higher taxes that depress business confidence, and so firms cut investment.

    B. Higher public spending forces the central bank to print more money, creating inflation that reduces real investment.

    C. Higher public spending does not raise total output in the short run.

    D. Higher public spending leads to more public borrowing, depressing the supply of loanable funds and increasing the real interest rate, pushing firms to lower investment.

49. Which of the following is a tool of indirect finance?

A. Crowd-funding
B. A newly issued corporate bond
C. A bank loan
D. A stock

50. A reason why the Federal Reserve decided to abandon the use of monetary aggregates as intermediate targets is that the money multiplier

A. is stable through time.
B. is not responsive to the Federal Reserve's actions.
C. can sharply drop in periods of banking and financial crises.
D. is sensitive to changes of the US Treasury monetary liabilities.

51. Which of the following best describes demand-pull inflation?

A. A continual increase of the price level due to misguided expansionary policies
B. Inflation that is due to a decline in the rate of growth of money supply
C. Inflation that is due to a temporary increase in the cost of material or cost of labor
D. A once and for all increase in the price level due to a new collective bargaining contract

52. Which of the following actions would help a mutual fund maintain its liquidity when faced with an unusually high volume of withdrawals?

A. Purchase Treasury securities on the open market.
B. Sell assets at a distressed or fire sale price.
C. Apply for primary credit at the Federal Reserve Bank.
D. Ask its liquidity managers to focus on capital adequacy management until the crisis is over.

53. Which of the following events were NOT among the factors behind the financial crisis of 2008/2009?

A. Financial innovations like the securitization of sub-prime mortgages
B. Tight monetary policy in the 2003–2006 period
C. Declining business standards in mortgage loans origination
D. Conflict of interest at credit-rating agencies

54. Which of the following economic indicators can be used to measure the inflation rate?

A. The Personal Consumption Expenditures deflator
B. Labor force
C. Employment
D. Gross domestic product

55. Which of the following was NOT a reason for the expansion of US banking operations abroad?

A. The expansion of multinational corporations
B. The narrow focus of banking activities in foreign countries
C. The expansion of US firms' involvement with global trade
D. The stricter regulatory environment of the United States

56. According to the Keynesian "liquidity preference theory" of money demand, an increase in nominal income would

A. increase the demand for money, lowering the interest rate.
B. leave the demand for money unaltered but increase the interest rate.
C. decrease the demand for money but leave the interest rate unaltered.
D. increase the demand for money, raising the interest rate.

57. Which of the following statements best describes how the International Monetary Fund finances its loans during sovereign debt crises?

A. Member countries are assigned quotas proportional to the size of their economy and, in times of crises, the Fund can also borrow from member countries' accounts.
B. The Fund collects voluntary contributions in hard currency or gold from member countries.
C. The central banks of the largest industrialized countries contribute 20 percent of their foreign reserves.
D. Monthly, the Fund borrows on the open market the funds needed, with a majority of the funds borrowed being denominated in dollars, euros, or yens.

58. In which of the following cases does targeting inflation prevent the central bank from achieving its dual goal of price stability and maximum sustainable employment?

A. When the economy is subject to a sustained increase in total spending

B. When the economy is subject to a sustained decrease in total spending

C. When the economy suffers from a permanent decline in potential output

D. When the economy is subject to a temporary increase in the price of oil or the cost of labor

59. The Glass-Steagall Act, also known as the Banking Act of 1933, imposed several types of regulations on the banking sector. For example, it

A. prohibited commercial banks from engaging in nonbank activities like underwriting insurance.

B. allowed banks to pay interest to holders of checkable deposits.

C. prohibited gender and racial discrimination in credit transactions.

D. allowed the Comptroller of the Currency to charter national banks.

60. If an accommodating monetary policy of the central bank successfully lowers interest rates, we should expect a

A. depreciation of the domestic currency.

B. decline in consumption expenditures.

C. decline in asset prices.

D. decline in inflation expectations

ANSWER KEY AND EXPLANATIONS

1. A	13. B	25. B	37. B	49. C
2. D	14. A	26. B	38. C	50. C
3. B	15. B	27. D	39. D	51. A
4. C	16. D	28. B	40. C	52. B
5. D	17. A	29. D	41. B	53. B
6. A	18. B	30. A	42. A	54. A
7. A	19. D	31. B	43. B	55. B
8. C	20. A	32. B	44. B	56. D
9. C	21. D	33. D	45. D	57. A
10. B	22. D	34. B	46. D	58. D
11. C	23. D	35. A	47. B	59. A
12. A	24. C	36. A	48. D	60. A

1. **The correct answer is A.** In the United States, reserve requirements are decided by the Board of Governors of the Federal Reserve System. The FOMC (choice B) decides the target level for the Federal Funds Rate, not reserve requirements. The Office of the Comptroller of the Currency (choice C) charters and regulates national banks but does not set reserve requirements. The FDIC (choice D) helps prevent bank runs by insuring bank depositors up to $250,000 per insured bank.

2. **The correct answer is D.** An authority provides liquidity guarantee if it can inject liquidity and act as a lender of last resort; an authority provides credit guarantees if it insures deposit accounts. In the United States, these functions belong to the Federal Reserve Bank and the FDIC. Choice A is incorrect because the OCC and state agencies charter and regulate commercial banks but do not provide liquidity or credit guarantees. Choice B is incorrect because the OCC does not provide liquidity guarantees. Choice C is incorrect because the OCC does not provide credit guarantees.

3. The correct answer is B. If the central bank wants to maintain the interest rate stability, it must inject reserves when the economy is strong and family and businesses want to borrow and drain resources when the economy is weak. Choice A is incorrect because the central bank can target the money supply or the interest rate but not both. Choice C is incorrect because if the central bank drains resources when there is a higher demand for credit, the interest rate increases. Choice D is incorrect because banks' willingness to lend is not sensitive to the central bank's choice of target.

4. The correct answer is C. Asset transformation is the activity of transforming a bank's liabilities into assets, for example, transforming deposited funds into a loan. Choice A is incorrect because a repo affects liabilities only. Choice B is incorrect because the choosing of stocks to include in a mutual fund does not transform liabilities into assets. Choice D is incorrect because selling one type of assets to purchase another is called asset management, not asset transformation.

5. The correct answer is D. When central banks cannot influence bank lending by lowering the policy rate, they try to obtain the same result with massive injections of reserves. Choice A is incorrect because buying securities from the Treasury does not stimulate lending. Choice B describes the practice of supplying "easy credit." Choice C describes a different unconventional tool of monetary policy.

6. The correct answer is A. The FDIC does not cover investment accounts, life insurance products, securities, stocks, bonds, and other products offered by banks. The FDIC insures all deposit accounts, including money market deposit accounts (choice B), certificates of deposit (choice C), and savings accounts (choice D).

7. **The correct answer is A.** Monetarists and Keynesians agree that monetary policy can stimulate the economy by affecting credit conditions and the interest rate if investment is sensitive to credit conditions and interest rates. Choice B is incorrect because Keynesians believe that expansionary policy is less effective when consumption is not sensitive to current disposable income. Choice C is incorrect because if the central bank has little control over interest rates, it finds it hard to stimulate investment and total spending. Choice D is incorrect because, in the long run, monetary policy is neutral, and it has no effect on total output.

8. **The correct answer is C.** The US monetary policy is decided by the FOMC, and the seven members of the Board of Governors are voting members of the FOMC. Choice A is incorrect because banking supervision is not an activity related to monetary policy. Choice B is incorrect because the Board of Governors creates and publishes economic data; however, this activity is not one aspect of monetary policy. Choice D is incorrect because the FOMC chooses the target level for the Federal Funds Rate.

9. **The correct answer is C.** Under a whole bank purchase and assumption agreement, all assets and liabilities of the failing bank are transferred to the assuming bank for a onetime payment. Choice A is incorrect because under a payoff and dissolve approach, the FDIC pays off depositors and then liquidates all assets and uses the sale's proceeds to pay off other creditors. Choice B is incorrect because no approach to the resolution of a failing bank is called liquidate and resolve. Choice D is incorrect because under a clean bank purchase and assumption approach, the assuming bank acquires only insured deposits and few assets or, in other words, a clean bank.

10. **The correct answer is B.** An open market purchase of Treasury securities injects reserves in the banking system and increases the monetary base, leading to a higher money supply. Choice A is incorrect because a higher interest on reserves would reduce the amount of reserves banks wish to loan out, reducing the money multiplier and the money supply. Choice C is incorrect because a higher discount rate raises the amount of excess reserve banks wish to hold, reducing the money multiplier and the money supply. Choice D is incorrect because a higher required reserve ratio would lower the money multiplier and money supply.

11. **The correct answer is C.** In the Balance of Payment, inflows of payments are recorded as credits and earnings payments are tallied in the current account. Choice A is incorrect because the financial account tallies payments from the purchase and sale of financial assets. Choice B is incorrect because the capital account tallies payments from the purchase and sale of nonfinancial assets. Choice D is incorrect because an inflow of payments is tallied as a credit.

12. **The correct answer is A.** The Economic Recovery Act of October 2008 authorized the Treasury to inject $700 billion into the shadow banking system to prop up its capitalization. Choice B is incorrect because the Federal Reserve set up the Term Auction Facilities to lower the stigma associated with borrowing funds from the Fed. Choice C is incorrect because the Federal Reserve extended loans to AIG. Choice D is incorrect because the Bear Stearns deal was brokered by the Federal Reserve.

13. **The correct answer is B.** Monetarists believed that only monetary policy could sway total spending. They also believed it did so with long lags, hence discretionary policy could destabilize the economy and they favored strict rules. Choice A is incorrect because monetarists believed fiscal policy had no effect on total spending. Choice C is incorrect because they believed that monetary policy was the only policy that could influence total spending. Choice D is incorrect because they feared that discretionary monetary policy would lead to higher inflation.

14. **The correct answer is A.** The Federal Reserve System is composed of twelve regional Reserve Banks, the Board of Governors, and the Federal Open Market Committee (FOMC). Choice B is incorrect because the Federal Deposit Insurance Corporation (FDIC) is not part of the Federal Reserve System. Choice C is incorrect because there are twelve regional Reserve Banks in the Federal Reserve System. Choice D is incorrect because there are twelve regional Reserve Banks in the Federal Reserve System and the FDIC is not part of the system.

15. **The correct answer is B.** You use money as a standard of deferred payment when you agree money can be used to settle a debt. A store of value (choice A) is when you store money for future purchases. A unit of account (choice C) is when you measure prices in cash units. A means of payment (choice D) is when you use money for a current purchase.

16. **The correct answer is D.** The Riegle-Neal Interstate Banking Act of 1994 removed the restrictions on nationwide branching. Choice A is incorrect because Regulation Q, introduced by the Glass-Steagall Act, imposed limits on interest paid on various deposits and prohibited paying interest on demand deposits. The McFadden Act of 1927 (choice B) required national banks to open branches only according to the laws of the state where they were located, effectively prohibiting national branching. The DIDMCA (choice C) did not prohibit nationwide branching but, among other things, lifted restrictions on interest paid on deposits.

17. **The correct answer is A.** A lower primary credit rate reduces banks' cost of using Fed loans to raise liquidity, leading to an increase in Fed loans and the borrowed monetary base. Choice B is incorrect because banks would buy more securities from the Fed if the Fed performed an open market purchase of securities. Choice C is incorrect because a lower discount rate leads banks to hold fewer excess resources, increasing the size of the money multiplier. Choice D is incorrect because when the public holds less currency, the money multiplier increases.

18. **The correct answer is B.** An asset is liquid when it can be easily turned into cash. Checkable deposits can be turned into cash with no limits and restrictions. Choice A is incorrect because it takes time to cash in a plot of land. Choice C is incorrect because, while shares in money market mutual funds can be cashed in without penalties, it takes time to do so. Choice D is incorrect because banks impose restrictions on withdrawals from savings accounts.

19. **The correct answer is D.** A higher required reserve ratio lowers the money supply, as it forces banks to keep a larger share of deposits as reserves, reducing the amount of excess reserves banks can loan out. Choice A is incorrect because banks do not close depositors' accounts to comply with reserve requirements. Choice B is incorrect because a higher required reserve ratio lowers the money supply. Choice C is incorrect because a higher required reserve ratio lowers the money supply.

20. **The correct answer is A.** Bank examiners rate banks according to the soundness and adequacy of their capital, assets, management, earnings, liquidity, and sensitivity to risk. Choices B, C, and D are incorrect because none of them is a dimension of the CAMELS rating system.

21. **The correct answer is D.** During a bank crisis, depositors' withdrawals drastically increase banks' obligations, forcing banks to stop renewing expiring loans (they call in loans) to create some liquidity. As a result, money supply sharply declines. The Federal Reserve can prevent this outcome by injecting liquidity and raising the monetary base. Choice A is incorrect because the increase in currency in circulation less than compensates the decline in deposits and money supply declines. Choice B is incorrect because when depositors withdraw funds total reserves decline and so do excess reserves. Choice C is incorrect because depositor's withdrawals do not affect the Fed's balance sheet or the monetary base.

22. **The correct answer is D.** When investors adapt their expectations slowly, they have adaptive expectations. When investors have rational expectations (choice A), they use all information efficiently and adapt their expectations very fast. Hyperbolic expectations (choice B) are not relevant economic concepts. Choice C is incorrect because even if investors are slow in responding to changes in economic variable, the name is adaptive expectations.

23. **The correct answer is D.** Through bank failures and mergers, the overall number of commercial banks has declined from more than 30,000 in 1920 to around 5,000 today. However, the number of branches has increased. Choice A is incorrect because the number of commercial banks has not increased. Choice B is incorrect because while today there are about 5,000 commercial banks, the number of banks has declined over the last century. Choice C is incorrect because the number of banks has been declining over the entire century.

24. **The correct answer is C.** The equation of exchange is at the heart of the quantity theory of money, and it states that the stock of money in the economy times the velocity of money is equal to income at current prices or, in economic parlance, to the nominal value of output. Choice A is incorrect because the current account and the financial account sum to the negative of the capital account. Choice B is incorrect because the statement describes the purchase power parity theory, not the equation of exchange. Choice D is incorrect because the statement describes the law of one price, not the equation of exchange.

25. **The correct answer is B.** Checkable deposits are counted in M1 and in M2, while shares in money market mutual funds are counted in M2 only. Moving $1,000 from a mutual fund to a checkable deposit raises M1 and leaves M2 the same.

26. The correct answer is B. Commercial banks are stock-owned, while credit unions are mutual institutions. Choice A is incorrect because both commercial banks and credit unions are depository institutions allowed to accept deposits; deposits at credit unions are called shares. Choice C is incorrect because credit unions are rather small because depositors must share a common bond. Choice D is incorrect because commercial banks are supervised by states and the Comptroller of the Currency, while credit unions are supervised by the National Credit Union Association.

27. The correct answer is D. Gross domestic product is a measure of total output and is the sum of consumption, investment, government purchases, and net exports. Choice A is incorrect because the sum of consumption and saving is disposable income, which is total income minus net taxes. Choice B is incorrect because disposable income and net taxes sum up to net national income that, unlike GDP, doesn't count capital depreciation. Choice C is incorrect because net taxes are not a component of GDP.

28. The correct answer is B. Loans represent about 55 percent of commercial banks' total assets. Equity capital (choice A) is the bank's net worth, which is the difference between the bank's assets and the bank's liabilities. Security investments (choice C) represent less than 20 percent of commercial banks' total assets. Deposits (choice D) are the larger share of commercial banks' liabilities.

29. The correct answer is D. Classical economists believe that prices and the economy operate at full employment all the time. Keynesian economists believe that prices are sticky, but the economy re-adjusts to potential output over time. Choice A is incorrect because Keynesian economists believe that prices are sticky in the short run. Choice B is incorrect because Keynesian economists believe that higher government spending can help maintain the economy at full employment. Choice C is incorrect because both classical and Keynesian economists believe that monetary policy can help maintain price stability.

30. **The correct answer is A.** The Basel 1 agreement made capital requirements sensitive to risk exposure, so that currently banks must have a leverage ratio of more than 3 percent and a ratio of Tier 1 and Tier 2 capital to risk-weighted assets of at least 8 percent. Choice B is incorrect because regulation requires a leverage ratio higher than 3 percent. Choice C is incorrect because capital regulation focuses on the ratio of capital to assets. Choice D is incorrect because capital regulation focuses on the ratio of capital to assets.

31. **The correct answer is B.** When inflation increases, the central bank responds by increasing the real interest rate, which dampens investment and total spending. Choice A is incorrect because when real wages decline, firms hire more workers. Choice C is incorrect because inflation does not necessarily lower business confidence. Choice D is incorrect because a slower pace of technological change does not lead to lower spending.

32. **The correct answer is B.** The CRA is the Community Reinvestment Act that requires banks to extend loans to customers from all neighborhoods in their market and pushes banks to extend loans to families that have a high risk of default. Choice A is incorrect because banks are now allowed to pay interest on demand deposits. Choice C is incorrect because the type of moral hazard described is an unintended consequence of insuring deposit accounts. Choice D is incorrect because the SEC is responsible for accounting rules.

33. **The correct answer is D.** If economic agents have rational expectations, they anticipate the long-term effects of fiscal policy on prices and inflation and act accordingly, thereby keeping the GDP and employment levels at an equilibrium for both the long- and short-run. Choice A is incorrect because rational expectations agents correctly anticipate the policy's effect on prices and inflation speeding up the policy lag of monetary policy. Choice B is incorrect because if economic agents have rational expectations expansionary policies are more likely to create demand pull inflation. Choice C is incorrect because if economic agents have rational expectations, a misguided expansionary policy or an increase in the cost of material can easily trigger cost push inflation.

34. **The correct answer is B.** It takes about two years for a change in the federal funds rate to fully affect total spending. Choice A is incorrect because the central bank has significant control over short-term interest rates. Choice C is incorrect because the central bank can immediately change the federal funds rate. Choice D is incorrect because investment and consumption, two key components of total spending, are sensitive to the interest rate.

35. **The correct answer is A.** The Acts allowed national banks to issue tax-free notes, and it increased state banks' reliance on demand deposits. With no reserve requirements or deposit insurance, bank runs and bank panics became very frequent. Choice B is incorrect because the US banking system is still a dual system with state and national banks. Choice C is incorrect because the number of currencies declined and soon only notes issued by national banks and backed by Treasury securities were used as money, but this was a positive consequence of the Acts. Choice D is incorrect because the National Bank Acts were passed in the 1860s, while the Federal Reserve Bank was created pursuant the Federal Reserve Act of 1913.

36. **The correct answer is A.** The FDIC was established by the Banking Act of 1933, also known as the Glass-Steagall Act. Choice B is incorrect because the Federal Reserve Act was signed in 1913. Choice C is incorrect because the Federal Reserve Act of 1913 established the Federal Reserve Bank. Choice D is incorrect because the McFadden Act was signed in 1927 and did not establish the FDIC.

37. **The correct answer is B.** The First Bank of the United States was established by Congress in 1781 at the urging of Alexander Hamilton, who believed a national bank could improve credit, tax collection, and business in the Union. Andrew Jackson (choice A) represented the interests of the agrarian states and was opposed to the idea of a National Bank. John Maynard Keynes (choice C) was a British economist who lived in the twentieth century. Milton Friedman (choice D) was the most important monetarist who lived in the twentieth century.

38. **The correct answer is C.** Banks engage in interest-based activities, like lending, and in fee-based activities of pure intermediation; these activities have no influence on the banks' balance sheet and hence are called off-balance sheet activities. Originating loans for resale is one such activity. Choice A is incorrect because loans held to maturity are assets recorded in banks' balance sheets. Choice B is incorrect because excess reserves are assets recorded in the banks' balance sheet. Choice D is incorrect because, while securitization is an off-balance sheet activity, holding mortgage-backed securities is an on-balance sheet activity.

39. **The correct answer is D.** A country that allows inflows and outflows of financial capital can maintain the foreign exchange rate at a chosen parity only by forcing its interest rate to follow the interest rate in the rest of the world, effectively losing control of its monetary policy. Choice A is incorrect because the United States is a democratic country with a trade balance deficit that allows its currency to float against foreign currencies. Choice B is incorrect because countries that run a public deficit generally also suffer from a balance of trade deficit. Choice C is incorrect because the United States can have an open economy and the Federal Reserve can use any of the tools of monetary policy.

40. **The correct answer is C.** The President of each Regional Reserve Bank is elected by six of the nine members of the Bank's Board of Directors. The Board of Governors chooses three of these six voting members. Choice A is incorrect because the Board of Governors does not directly appoint the regional Reserve Banks' Presidents. Choice B is incorrect because the President of the United States appoints the members of the Board of Governors, not the Presidents of the regional Feds. Choice D is incorrect because the Board of Governors does not make recommendations to the Board of Directors.

41. The correct answer is B. The interbank rate, the interest rate banks charge each other on short-term loans, is not a tool of monetary policy but a policy instrument and an operational target. Large-scale asset purchases (choice A), also known as quantitative easing, are unconventional tools of monetary policy. The interest on reserves (choice C) is a tool of monetary policy. The discount rate (choice D) is a tool of monetary policy.

42. The correct answer is A. Real variables focus on the purchase power of their nominal counterparts, hence the real interest rate is the difference between the market rate and the change in price people expect. The difference between the market rate and the cost of money (choice B) is an indicator of banks' profitability. The interest rate on mortgages or auto loans (choice C) is a nominal variable. The difference between the domestic and foreign rates (choice D) is an indicator of future movements of the foreign exchange rates.

43. The correct answer is B. An open market purchase of securities injects reserves into the banking system, raising the monetary base and the money supply. Choice A is incorrect because an increase in the monetary base leads to higher money supply. Choice C is incorrect because an open market purchase of securities increases the monetary base. Choice D is incorrect because an open market purchase of securities increases the monetary base, which increases the money supply.

44. The correct answer is B. Starting in 2009, banks are holding trillions in excess reserves and the equilibrium federal funds rate is close to or lower than the interest on reserves. To raise the federal funds rate, the Federal Reserve can rely on changes in the interest on reserves. Choice A is incorrect because after 2009 an outright sale of Treasury security could not raise the federal funds rate. Choice C is incorrect because lowering the required reserve ratio depresses the federal funds rate. Choice D is incorrect because the FOMC has no authority over the primary discount rate.

45. **The correct answer is D.** Purchases of Treasury securities on the open market are a tool of monetary policy. Choice A is incorrect because unemployment benefits are one type of transfer, and their automatic increase during downturns is an example of an automatic stabilizer. Choice B is incorrect because a temporary reduction in taxes is a tool of fiscal policy. Choice C is incorrect because grants to states to finance government purchases are a tool of fiscal policy.

46. **The correct answer is D.** The purchase power parity theory applies the law of one price to international trade. If it's cheaper to buy an item domestically than import it from abroad, then exports will increase, imports will drop, and the foreign exchange will adjust, returning parity to the domestic and international price. Choice A is incorrect because the purchase power parity theory applies the law of one price to international trade. Choice B is incorrect because the depreciation of the currency does not necessarily lead to higher wages. Choice C is incorrect because it states the main point of the interest rate parity theory.

47. **The correct answer is B.** In the 1930s, the frequency of bank panics and bank runs fell only after the FDIC was created and started insuring bank deposits. Choice A is incorrect because in a bank crisis it is the Federal Reserve that can inject liquidity and act as lender of last resort. Choice C is incorrect because the FDIC uses several methods to resolve failing banks. Choice D is incorrect because the FDIC does not regulate capital requirements.

48. **The correct answer is D.** The key idea of crowding out is that government and the private sector compete for funds so that when government absorbs more funds, fewer are available to finance private investment. Choice A is incorrect because higher public spending creates expectations of a stronger economy, boosting business confidence. Choice B is incorrect because if the central bank increases money supply, the interest rate declines, boosting investment. Choice C is incorrect because the "crowding out" effect is a long-run phenomenon.

49. The correct answer is C. Indirect finance channels funds from investors to users through financial intermediaries. A bank loan is a tool of indirect finance as it is intermediated by a bank. In crowd-funding (choice A), the funds move directly from holders to users. Choice B is incorrect because when an investor buys a newly issued corporate bond, the funds flow directly to their user. Choice D is incorrect because when a corporation issues new stock, the funds flow directly to their user.

50. The correct answer is C. The money multiplier is sensitive to the currency ratio and the excess reserve ratio that are not stable through time. Choice A is incorrect because evidence from the years following the financial crises shows a decline of the money multiplier. Choice B is incorrect because a change in the discount rate or the interest paid on reserves can influence the excess reserve ratio and the money multiplier. Choice D is incorrect because changes in the US Treasury monetary liabilities affect the monetary base but do not affect the money multiplier.

51. The correct answer is A. If policy makers unwittingly try to keep the unemployment rate below its natural level, they repeatedly stimulate spending, triggering demand-pull inflation. Choice B is incorrect because a decline in the rate of growth of money supply slows inflation. Choice C describes cost-push inflation. Choice D is incorrect because inflation is a continual increase of the price level.

52. The correct answer is B. In a liquidity crisis, a mutual fund can sell some of its assets at a price below its intrinsic value (fire sale) to increase cash at hand. Choice A is incorrect because buying securities exacerbates the fund's liquidity problem. Choice C is incorrect because only depository institutions can apply for primary credit at the Fed. Choice D is incorrect because the fund has a liquidity problem and should not divert resources away from the liquidity management division into the capital management division.

53. **The correct answer is B.** In the 2003–2006 period, monetary policy was accommodating. In fact, some economists believe that this accommodating stance fueled the housing bubble at the heart of the financial crisis. Choice A is incorrect because financial innovation like securitization dramatically increased funds availability in the housing market fueling the market bubble. Choice C is incorrect because declining business standards at mortgage originators lowered the quality and raised the risk of the mortgages backing the new securities, injecting risk in the financial sector. Choice D is incorrect because credit agencies' new practice of advising firms on how to structure new complex financial instruments created a conflict of interest that led them to give these instruments inaccurately high ratings.

54. **The correct answer is A.** Inflation is a continual increase of the price level. To measure inflation, economists use a price indicator like the Personal Consumption Expenditures deflator. The labor force (choice B) counts employed and unemployed workers. Employment (choice C) counts all workers who hold a job. Gross domestic product (choice D) is a measure of total output.

55. **The correct answer is B.** In foreign countries, commercial banks have always been allowed to engage in a broader range of financial activities, such as offering life insurance. Choice A is incorrect because US banks expanded their operations abroad in response to the expansion of multinational corporations. Choice C is incorrect because US banks expanded their operations abroad to help their business clients import supplies and parts from abroad and sell their final product to foreign countries. Choice D is incorrect because US banks expanded their operations abroad to evade some of the strict regulations that characterize the US banking sector, such as the separation between commercial and investment banking.

56. **The correct answer is D.** People hold money to pay for transactions and as a store of values. An increase in nominal income raises the demand for money held for transaction purposes, and the interest rate must increase to keep the money market in equilibrium. Choice A is incorrect because a higher money demand leads to higher interest rates. Choice B is incorrect because a higher nominal income raises the money demand. Choice C is incorrect because a higher income leads to a higher demand for money and because a decline in the demand for money would lower the interest rate.

57. **The correct answer is A.** During debt crises, the IMF can expand its ability to act as a lender of last resort by borrowing from member countries. Choice B is incorrect because membership is contingent on the payment of fixed quotas. Choice C is incorrect because all member countries must contribute. Choice D is incorrect because the funds are not borrowed on the open market, but deposited by member countries.

58. **The correct answer is D.** A temporary increase in the cost of production lowers output below potential and triggers cost-pushed inflation. If the central bank raises interest rates to prevent higher inflation, it depresses investment and consumption, deepening the recession and creating higher unemployment. Choice A is incorrect because higher total spending leads to higher inflation and output above potential. If the central bank raises interest rates to prevent higher inflation, it depresses total spending, cooling off the economy. Choice B is incorrect because lower total spending leads to lower inflation and lower output. If the central bank lowers interest rates to prevent higher inflation, it stimulates total spending, closing the output gap. Choice C is incorrect because a permanent decline in potential output triggers higher inflation but does not create an output gap.

59. **The correct answer is A.** The Glass-Steagall Act limited commercial banks securities and insurance activities. Choice B is incorrect because the Glass-Steagall Act prohibited paying interest on demand deposits. Choice C is incorrect because discrimination in lending is outlawed by the Equal Credit Opportunity Act. Choice D is incorrect because national banks were introduced by the National Bank Acts of the mid-1800s.

60. **The correct answer is A.** A decline in the domestic interest rate lowers the relative demand for domestic securities and the relative demand for the domestic currency, leading to a depreciation of the domestic currency. Choice B is incorrect because lower interest rates stimulate consumption spending. Choice C is incorrect because an accommodating monetary policy raises asset prices. Choice D is incorrect because an accommodating monetary policy raises inflation expectations.

Like what you see? Get unlimited access to Peterson's full catalog of DSST practice tests, instructional videos, flashcards, and more for **75% off the first month!** Go to **www.petersons.com/testprep/dsst** and use coupon code **DSST2020** at checkout. Offer expires July 1, 2021.

CPSIA information can be obtained
at www.ICGtesting.com
Printed in the USA
JSHW041545070222
22644JS00007B/191